PIPE FITTINGS

NIPPLES

PIPE LENGTHS UP TO 22 FT.

STRAIGHT COUPLING

REDUCING COUPLING

T5-BBL-792

CAP

STRAIGHT TEE

REDUCING TEE

STREET TEE

STRAIGHT CROSS

REDUCING CROSS

90° ELBOW

90° ELBOW

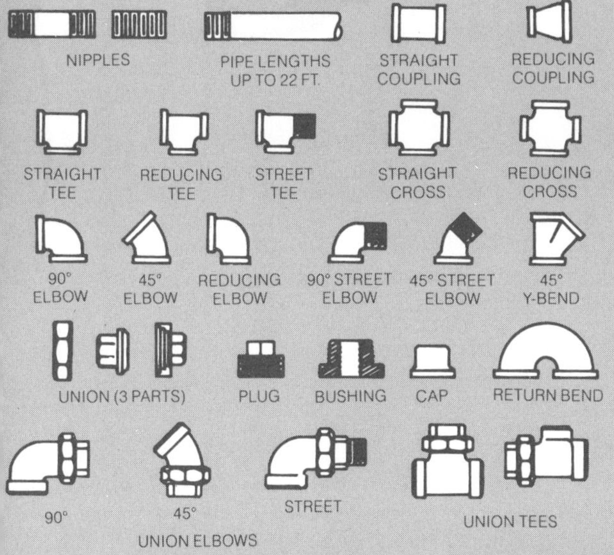

90° ELBOW · 45° ELBOW · REDUCING ELBOW · 90° STREET ELBOW · 45° STREET ELBOW · 45° Y-BEND

REDUCING TEE

REDUCER

UNION (3 PARTS)

PLUG

BUSHING

CAP

RETURN BEND

PLUG

45° ELBOW

TEE

90° · 45° · STREET

UNION ELBOWS · UNION TEES

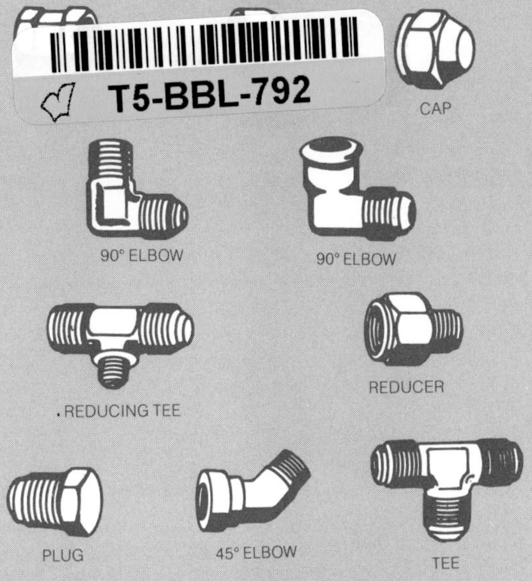

MEASURES OF CAPACITY

1 cup	=	8 fl oz
2 cups	=	1 pint
2 pints	=	1 quart
4 quarts	=	1 gallon
2 gallons	=	1 peck
4 pecks	=	1 bushel

STANDARD STEEL PIPE (All Dimensions in inches)

Nominal Size	Outside Diameter	Inside Diameter	Nominal Size	Outside Diameter	Inside Diameter
⅛	0.405	0.269	1	1.315	1.049
¼	0.540	0.364	1¼	1.660	1.380
⅜	0.675	0.493	1½	1.900	1.610
½	0.840	0.622	2	2.375	2.067
¾	1.050	0.824	2½	2.875	2.469

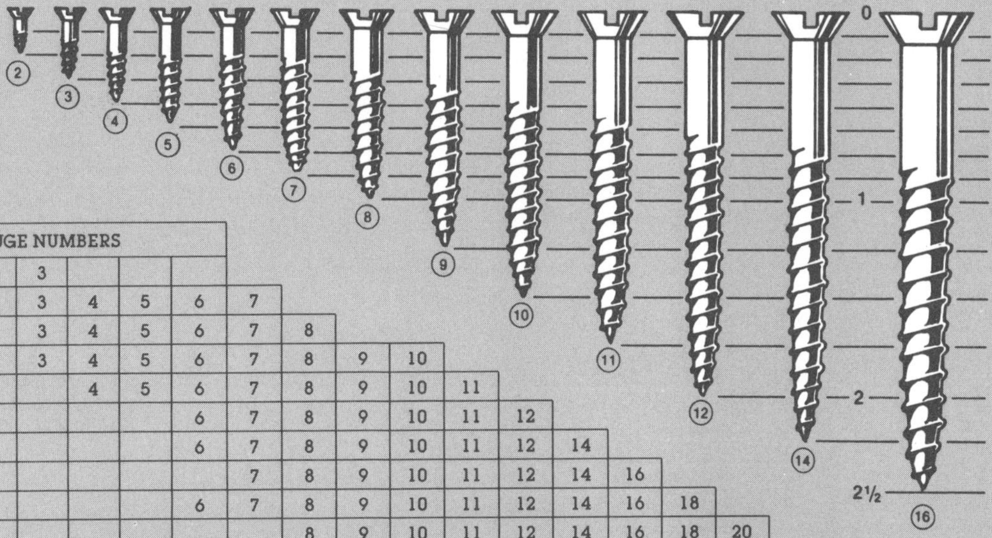

WOOD SCREWS

LENGTH	GAUGE NUMBERS														
¼ INCH	0	1	2	3											
⅜ INCH			2	3	4	5	6	7							
½ INCH			2	3	4	5	6	7	8						
⅝ INCH				3	4	5	6	7	8	9	10				
¾ INCH					4	5	6	7	8	9	10	11			
⅞ INCH							6	7	8	9	10	11	12		
1 INCH							6	7	8	9	10	11	12	14	
1¼ INCH								7	8	9	10	11	12	14	16
1½ INCH							6	7	8	9	10	11	12	14	16	18
1¾ INCH									8	9	10	11	12	14	16	18	20
2 INCH									8	9	10	11	12	14	16	18	20
2¼ INCH										9	10	11	12	14	16	18	20
2½ INCH													12	14	16	18	20
2¾ INCH														14	16	18	20
3 INCH															16	18	20
3½ INCH																18	20	24
4 INCH																18	20	24

WHEN YOU BUY SCREWS, SPECIFY (1) LENGTH, (2) GAUGE NUMBER, (3) TYPE OF HEAD—FLAT, ROUND, OR OVAL, (4) MATERIAL—STEEL, BRASS, BRONZE, ETC., (5) FINISH—BRIGHT, STEEL BLUED, CADMIUM, NICKEL, OR CHROMIUM PLATED.

Popular Mechanics

do-it-yourself encyclopedia

The complete, illustrated home reference guide from the world's most authoritative source for today's how-to-do-it information.

Volume 26

WEEKEND PROJECTS

to

WOODCARVING

HEARST DIRECT BOOKS

NEW YORK

Acknowledgements

The Popular Mechanics Encyclopedia is published with the consent and cooperation of POPULAR MECHANICS Magazine.

For POPULAR MECHANICS Magazine:

Editor-in-Chief: *Joe Oldham*
Managing Editor: *Bill Hartford*
Special Features Editor: *Sheldon M. Gallager*
Automotive Editor: *Wade A. Hoyt, SAE*
Home and Shop Editor: *Steve Willson*
Electronics Editor: *Stephen A. Booth*
Boating, Outdoors and Travel Editor: *Timothy H. Cole*
Science Editor: *Dennis Eskow*

Popular Mechanics Encyclopedia

Project Director: *Boyd Griffin*
Manufacturing: *Ron Schoenfeld*
Assistant Editors: *Cynthia W. Lockhart,
Peter McCann, Rosanna Petruccio*
Production Coordinator: *Peter McCann*

The staff of Popular Mechanics Encyclopedia is grateful to the following individuals and organizations:
Editor: *C. Edward Cavert*
Editor Emeritus: *Clifford B. Hicks*
Production: *Layla Productions*
Production Director: *Lori Stein*
Book Design: *The Bentwood Studio*
Art Director: *Jos. Trautwein*
Design Consultant: *Suzanne Bennett & Associates*
Illustrations: *AP Graphics, Evelyne Johnson Associates, Popular Mechanics Magazine, Vantage Art.*

Contributing Writers: Sam Allen, *Music you can make in your shop*, page 3219; Penelope Angell, *Layering wood: a fine art*, page 3294; *Bird carving secrets*, page 3314; *Woodcarving projects*, page 3318; Penelope Angell and Rosario Capotosto, *Veneering: beautiful wood on a budget*, page 3305; Manly Banister, *Bending wood*, page 3299; Walter E. Burton, *Cloth tape inlays*, page 3313; George Campbell, *Circus music from your shop*, page 3204; Rosario Capotosto, *Mail organizer*, page 3215; *Wine rack has handy tray*, page 3247; C. Wayne Close, *Key house number*, page 3213; James Finneran, *Carve these gulls in flight*, page 3317; Don Geary, *Windows: an introduction*, page 3227; Philip Hermann, *Glass cutting short course*, page 3245; R. Bruce Hoadley, *What is wood?*, page 3267; John H. Ingersoll, *Picking lumber*, page 3271; Harold Jackson, *Fun projects*, page 3213; W. Clyde Lammey, *Lumber basics for the craftsman*, page 3274; Wayne C. Leckey, *Cue-and-ball rack*, page 3215; *Woodworking tips*, page 3283; Dan A. Robertson, *Kaleidoscope dazzles everyone*, page 3210; Merton H. Slutz, *Swiss-cheese mountain game*, page 3215; Marc Stern, *Telephone installation*, page 3223; Jack Van Vleck, *Ski care*, page 3256; David A. Warren, *Woods and woodworking*, page 3261; Kenneth Wells, *Baffling puzzle*, page 3213; *Interlocking wood sculpture*; 3323.

Photographic Credits: Popular Mechanics Encyclopedia is grateful to the following for permission to reprint their photographs: Anderson Windows, page 3233; Caradco Corp., pages 3229 (top), 3230 (left); Certainteed, Inc., page 3228 (top); Hurd Windows, pages 3229 (bottom left and bottom right); K2 Corp., page 3256; Marvin Windows, pages 3227 and 3230 (top right); Olin Ski Co., page 3257; United Gilsonite Laboratories, page 3231; U.S. Dept. of Agriculture—Forest Service, Forest Products Laboratory, page 1 color insert; Universal Metal Products, page 3230 (bottom right); Vinyl Building Products, Inc., page 3232 (top); David Warren, pages 3262 (right), 3263 (top left and top right), 3264.

ISBN 0-87851-179-2

Library of Congress 85-81760

10 9 8 7 6 5 4 3 2 1

PRINTED IN THE UNITED STATES OF AMERICA

Although every effort has been made to ensure the accuracy and completeness of the information in this book, Hearst Direct Books makes no guarantees, stated or implied, nor will they be liable in the event of misinterpretation or human error made by the reader, or for any typographical errors that may appear. WORK SAFELY WITH HAND TOOLS. WEAR SAFETY GOGGLES. READ MANUFACTURER'S INSTRUCTIONS AND WARNINGS FOR ALL PRODUCTS.

Contents

Circus music from your shop

■ IF THE HAUNTING sounds of the circus bring back happy childhood memories, or if you have a budding musician in the family, a miniature calliope could be the perfect shop project for you. This little pipe organ, made from readily available materials, whistles with air from hair dryers built into the cabinet. Building the calliope should take about 40 hours.

To begin, cut the cabinet and wind-chest components—parts A through Q, T and U (see the materials list at the end of this article). Bore pilot holes for all screws connecting the cabinet parts with a No. 6 bit. Counterbore all pilot holes with a ⅜-in. bit to receive the plugs (V). Then lay out

WHEN YOU depress calliope keys, air from internal blowers rushes into pipes, producing tones that sound like an orchestra of flutes and whistles.

and bore guide holes in the keyboard base (E) and the rocker support (I).

A drill press or drill guide for your portable drill is a must for accuracy. Clamp together the top and bottom pieces of the wind chest (parts L and N) and bore them simultaneously so the holes will align. Use a depth stop to prevent boring through the bottom board. If you don't have a radial drill press or one with an adjustable table, bore the angled holes in the rocker support by using shims under the workpiece to establish the correct 5° angle.

Make a trial assembly of the chest. Once everything fits properly, sand and finish the cabinet and the screw hole plugs (V). You can use mahogany stain and finish the piece with varnish. When dry, remove wind chest, keyboard back (G), music rack (J), rocker support (I) and its cover (K).

Next, prepare the keyboard. Rip $\frac{7}{8}$-in. strips from the type wood used for the cabinet. Cut white keys (parts X_1, X_2, X_3 and X_4). Cut the black keys (Y) from $\frac{1}{2}$-in. molding stock. Bore pivot holes as accurately as possible through the sides of the keys. Then bore $\frac{1}{4}$-in. holes on the undersides of the keys for the guide pins (Z). Bore a $\frac{5}{16}$-in. dimple at the back of each key.

Sand all the keys smooth, removing a total of about $\frac{1}{32}$ in. from the width of each key to ensure proper clearance between them when they're in place. Install the guide pins and apply several coats of spray paint to the keys.

When the keys have dried, insert them through the keyboard back in order. Insert the pivot rod (BB) through the holes in the sides of the keys, slipping a felt washer onto the rod between each pair of keys. Between keys 12 and 13 (notes B and C), insert the center pivot support (CC). Attach the two end supports (DD2) and secure the assembly with the pivot rod nuts.

Attach a length of foam weatherstripping (EE) to the keyboard base and install the keyboard. Check that all keys move freely and make adjustments to the elongated guide holes where needed.

After the keyboard is set, install the two blowers (WW) in the cabinet. The hair dryers used in this project are a common item in second-hand stores, but if you can't find that type, similar units or commercial blowers will work.

Disconnect, and remove the heating elements from the hairdryers. Hook up wiring through the switch (YY, see wiring diagram). Bring power cord wire through the 3/16-in. hole in the panel (B). Knot the wire on the inside of the hole to prevent strain on the connections.

The rocker assembly

Next, begin work on the rockers. Cut the rockers (S) from $\frac{1}{2}$x$\frac{7}{8}$-in. molding. It's faster to bore pivot-rod holes and dimples before you cut the individual pieces. Sand the sides of the rockers smooth, then add the screw hooks (HH) and counterweights (II). Insert the pivot rod (BB) through the rockers and attach the support brackets (DD1).

Cut the push rods (AA) and install the rocker support (I) in the cabinet, threading the air hoses through the 1⅜-in. holes. Attach the height adjuster assembly (R), then insert the push rods making sure they seat in the keys' dimples.

Mount the rocker assembly on the support (I). Adjust the height of the keys individually by screws (FF) to level the keyboard in the "up" position. You may have to alter the lengths of some of the push rods, as well. When the keyboard is level, the rockers should rest at approximately 15° from the horizontal plane. Finally, install the angled guide pins (GG). Establish the proper clearance by screwing the hooks (HH) in or out as needed. Check to see that the rockers are moving freely.

The next phase is forming the pipes: Carefully follow the specs in the chart, particularly those concerning the sound-producing (D-shaped) notches. Use a hacksaw to cut the aluminum tubing and remove all burrs with a mill file. Bore the round air hole near the bottom of each pipe with a $\frac{5}{16}$-in. bit. Position a flue stopper of the correct size as noted in the chart and insert a cork in the bottom of each pipe as shown in the pipe-assembly detail. Test each pipe by blowing gently through the $\frac{5}{16}$-in. hole. Each pipe should make a clear note.

Air-release assemblies

Make the 25 air-release assemblies. Glue the felt pads (QQ) to the PVC discs (OO) with contact cement or other glue for non-porous surfaces. Fasten the hinge leaves (SS) to the bottom of the dowel (NN) and to the bottom of the wind chest with brads that come in the hinge package. Form the springs (TT) by cutting the heads off 1½-in. safety pins and bending ⅛-in. of each cut end with needle-nose pliers to create "ears." Reassemble the wind chest, leaving off the top, and caulk all the joints with silicone sealant.

Tie an 18-in. length of braided fishing line (KK) to the screw eye on top of each dowel and thread each through its matching nylon tubing guide (MM). Mount the top of the chest and caulk all the joints.

Completing the calliope

Insert the pipes through the holes in the top of the wind chest. Manipulate the air-release assemblies by pulling on the lines until each pipe

seats in the base and each felt pad seats over the round air hole. Glue felt strips to the back of the wind chest and install it in the cabinet. Be sure to tighten the screws enough to compress the felt and seal the chest.

Attach the air hoses of the dryers to the copper pipe reducers (XX) mounted to the front of the

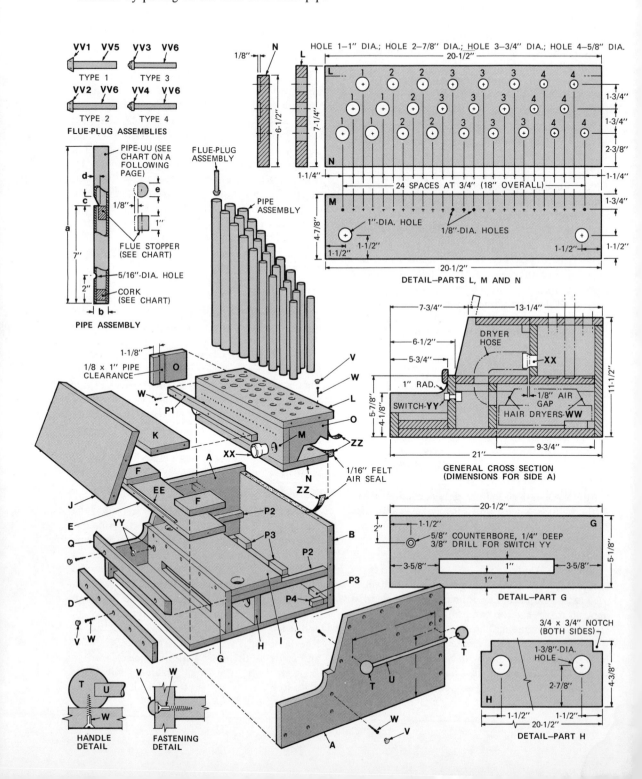

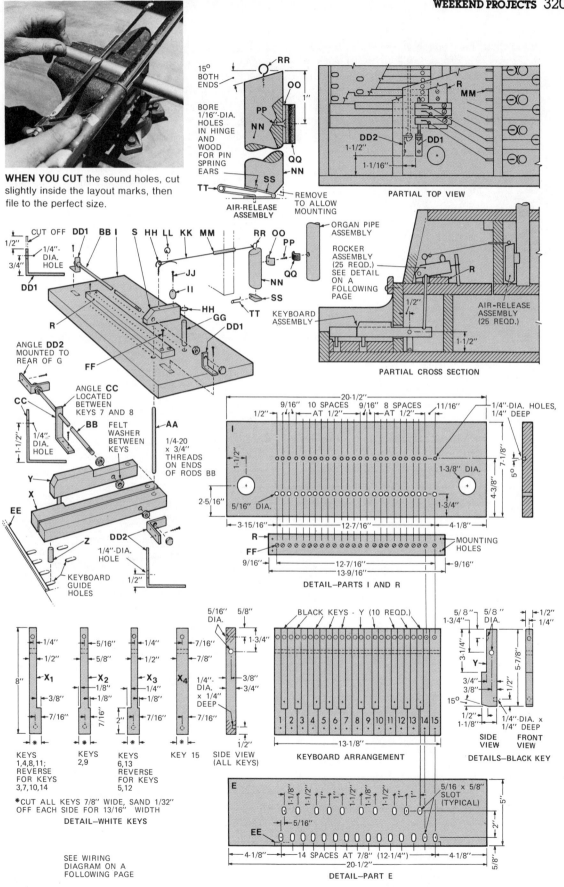

WHEN YOU CUT the sound holes, cut slightly inside the layout marks, then file to the perfect size.

15° BOTH ENDS

BORE 1/16"-DIA. HOLES IN HINGE AND WOOD FOR PIN SPRING EARS

RR
OO
1"
PP
NN
QQ
NN
SS
TT
AIR-RELEASE ASSEMBLY
REMOVE TO ALLOW MOUNTING

PARTIAL TOP VIEW
R
MM
DD2
1-1/2"
1-1/16"
DD1

CUT OFF
1/2"
1/4"-DIA. HOLE
3/4"
DD1
DD1
BB
S HH LL KK MM
RR OO
PP
ORGAN PIPE ASSEMBLY
ROCKER ASSEMBLY (25 REQD.) SEE DETAIL ON A FOLLOWING PAGE
R
JJ
NN
QQ
II
HH
GG
DD1
SS
TT
KEYBOARD ASSEMBLY
AIR-RELEASE ASSEMBLY (25 REQD.)
1/2"
1-1/2"
R
FF

ANGLE **DD2** MOUNTED TO REAR OF G

PARTIAL CROSS SECTION

ANGLE **CC** LOCATED BETWEEN KEYS 7 AND 8
CC
1-1/2"
1/4"-DIA. HOLE
BB
FELT WASHER BETWEEN KEYS
AA
1/4-20 x 3/4" THREADS ON ENDS OF RODS BB
Y
X
EE
Z
DD2
1/4"-DIA. HOLE
1/2"
KEYBOARD GUIDE HOLES

DETAIL—PARTS I AND R
20-1/2"
9/16" 10 SPACES 9/16" 8 SPACES 11/16"
1/2" AT 1/2" AT 1/2"
1/4"-DIA. HOLES, 1/4" DEEP
I
1-1/2"
7-1/8"
5°
1-3/8" DIA.
4-3/8"
2-5/16"
5/16" DIA.
1-3/4"
3-15/16"
12-7/16"
4-1/8"
R
FF
MOUNTING HOLES
9/16"
12-7/16"
9/16"
13-9/16"

DETAIL—WHITE KEYS

1/4"
1/2"
8"
X₁
3/8"
7/16"

5/16"
5/8"
X₂
1/8"
7/16"

1/4"
1/2"
X₃
1/8"
1/8"
2"
7/16"

7/16"
7/8"
X₄
7/16"

KEYS 1,4,8,11; REVERSE FOR KEYS 3,7,10,14

KEYS 2,9

KEYS 6,13 REVERSE FOR KEYS 5,12

KEY 15

5/16" DIA.
5/8"
1-3/4"
1/4"-DIA. x 1/4" DEEP
3/8"
3/4"
7/16"
1/2"
SIDE VIEW (ALL KEYS)

*CUT ALL KEYS 7/8" WIDE, SAND 1/32" OFF EACH SIDE FOR 13/16" WIDTH

BLACK KEYS - Y (10 REQD.)
1 2 3 4 5 6 7 8 9 10 11 12 13 14 15
13-1/8"
KEYBOARD ARRANGEMENT

5/8"
5/8" DIA.
1/2"
1/4"
1-3/4"
3-1/4"
Y
3/4"
3/8"
5-7/8"
1/2"
15°
1/2"
1/4"-DIA. x 1/4" DEEP
1-1/8"
SIDE VIEW
FRONT VIEW
DETAILS—BLACK KEY

SEE WIRING DIAGRAM ON A FOLLOWING PAGE

DETAIL—PART E
E
1-1/8" 1-1/2" 1-1/2" 1" 1" 1-1/2" 1-1/8" 1-1/2" 1-1/2"
5/16 x 5/8" SLOT (TYPICAL)
5"
2"
EE
5/16"
4-1/8"
14 SPACES AT 7/8" (12-1/4")
4-1/8"
20-1/2"
5/8"

wind chest. Turn on the dryers. By pulling on the lines, you should be able to make each pipe sound in turn. If any pipe produces a weak tone, enlarge the air hole to ⅜-in. dia.

Work in order, attaching the lines to the hooks on the rockers. Take two turns of the line around each hook, adjusting the line so it's tight, but doesn't lift the air-release assembly enough to let air enter the pipe. Crimp a split shot on the line to secure the adjustment.

Once all 25 lines are attached, test the action of the keyboard. If you find a sticky key (and you probably will at this point), loop a small rubber band around the base of the counterweight (II) and the rocker guide pin (GG).

Install the music rack (J), music stop (Q) and the rocker cover (K), then apply the screw hole buttons (Y). Finally, tune the pipes to a piano or other instrument, using the flue plugs in each pipe.

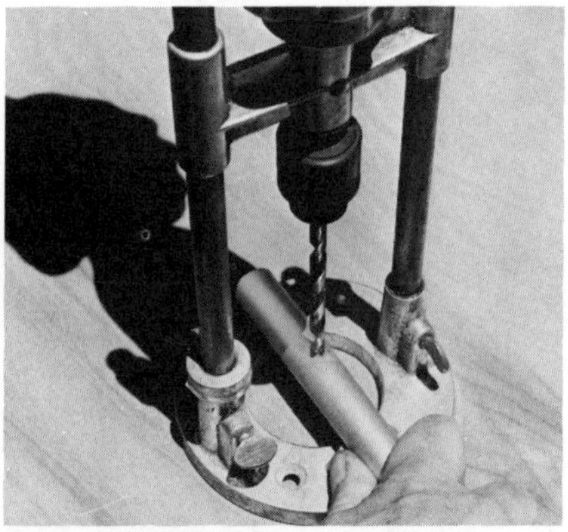

ROUND HOLES bored near the bottom of each pipe let air enter when keys are depressed. The ⁵⁄₁₆-in. holes may have to be enlarged if pipe tones are weak.

FLUE PLUG, flue stopper and cork above are shown outside the pipe, parallel to their actual positions when they are installed inside.

SPECIFICATIONS—CALLIOPE PIPES AND INTERNAL PARTS

Pipe No.	Length (a)	Outside Dia. (b)	NOTCH Height (c)	NOTCH Depth (d)	Flue Stopper Dowel o.d. (e)	Cork Size	Flue-Plug Type
1	21"	1"	⅝"	⁵⁄₁₆"	⅞"	10	1
2	20⅜	1	⅝	⁵⁄₁₆	⅞	10	1
3	19⅞	1	⅝	⁵⁄₁₆	⅞	10	1
4	19⅛	1	⅝	⁵⁄₁₆	⅞	10	1
5	18⅝	1	⅝	⁵⁄₁₆	⅞	10	1
6	18⅛	⅞	½	⁵⁄₁₆	¾	9	2
7	17⅝	⅞	½	⁵⁄₁₆	¾	9	2
8	17¼	⅞	½	⁵⁄₁₆	¾	9	2
9	16¾	⅞	½	⁵⁄₁₆	¾	9	2
10	16⅛	⅞	½	⁵⁄₁₆	¾	9	2
11	15⅝	¾	⁷⁄₁₆	¼	⅝	5	3
12	15⅛	¾	⁷⁄₁₆	¼	⅝	5	3
13	14¾	¾	⁷⁄₁₆	¼	⅝	5	3
14	14⅜	¾	⁷⁄₁₆	¼	⅝	5	3
15	14	¾	⁷⁄₁₆	¼	⅝	5	3
16	13¾	¾	⁷⁄₁₆	¼	⅝	5	3
17	13⅜	¾	⁷⁄₁₆	¼	⅝	5	3
18	13⅛	¾	⁷⁄₁₆	¼	⅝	5	3
19	12⅞	¾	⁷⁄₁₆	¼	⅝	5	3
20	12½	⅝	½	³⁄₁₆	½	3	4
21	12¼	⅝	½	³⁄₁₆	½	3	4
22	12	⅝	½	³⁄₁₆	½	3	4
23	11¾	⅝	½	³⁄₁₆	½	3	4
24	11½	⅝	½	³⁄₁₆	½	3	4
25	11¼	⅝	½	³⁄₁₆	½	3	4

CUT NO MORE than ⅛ in. from the dowels used for flue stoppers. The flat plane forces air out through the sound hole.

IF YOU DON'T have a band saw, use a table-mounted saber saw to cut keys. Good keyboard action requires accuracy.

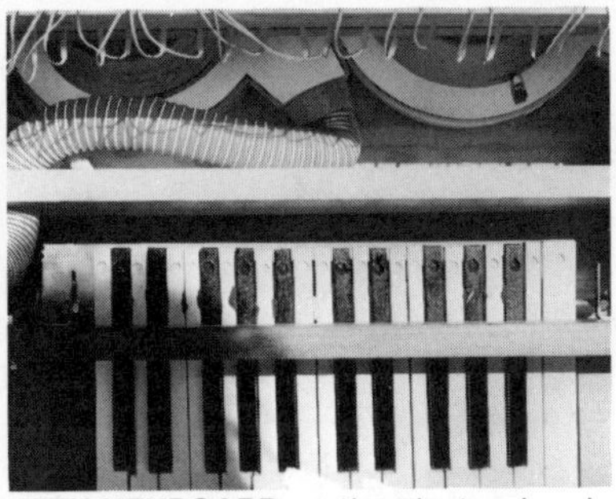

WITH KEYBOARD on the pivot rod and the wind chest and blowers in place, the keyboard must be leveled with adjustments to the guide holes.

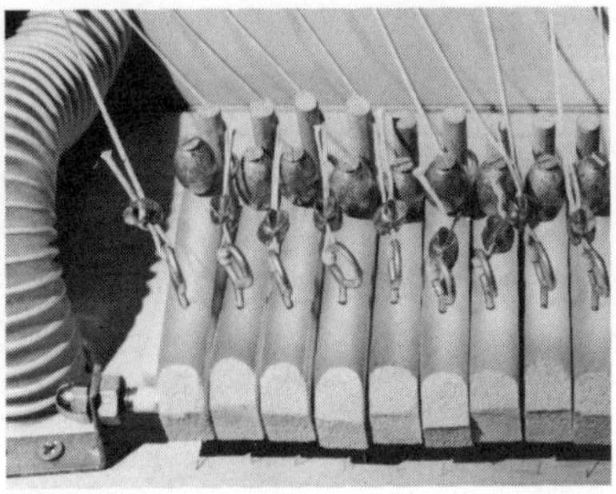

RIG LINES from the air-release assemblies to the rockers, using crimped split shots to maintain correct tension.

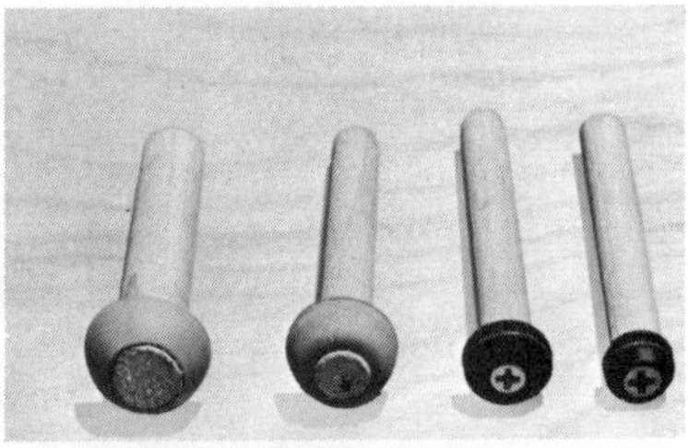

THE FLUE PLUGS are used to tune the pipes. Four different sizes are needed to fit the varying pipe diameters.

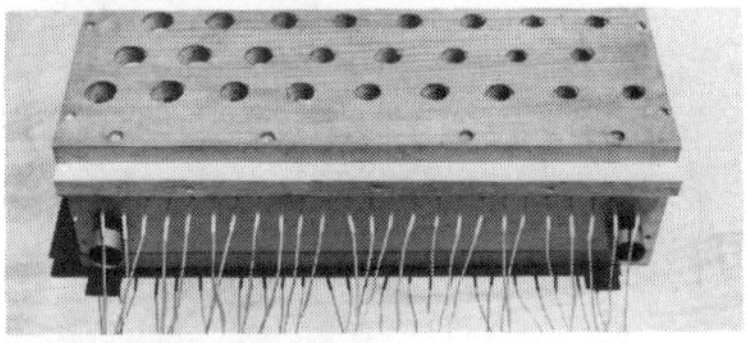

ASSEMBLED wind chest is shown above with lines for air-release assemblies threaded through nylon tubing guides.

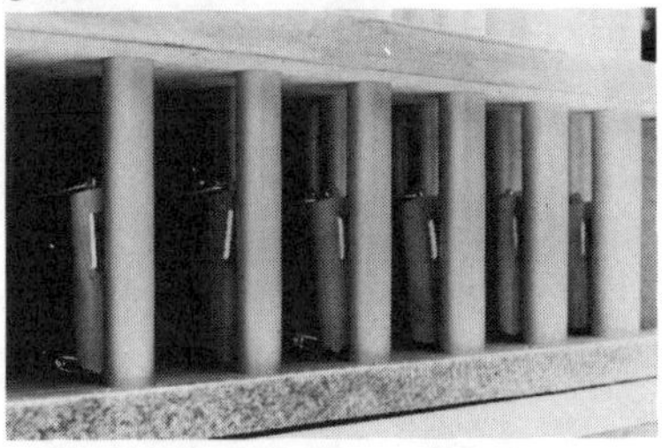

WITH PIPES inserted, the air-release assemblies are shown with the felt pads in place over the air holes. Check for correct alignment of all parts.

MATERIALS LIST—CALLIOPE

Key	No.	Size and description (use)
A	2	¾ x 11½ x 21" pine (cabinet sides)
B	1	¾ x 10¾ x 20½" pine (cabinet back)
C	1	¾ x 19½ x 20½" plywood (cabinet bottom)
D	1	¾ x 2¼ x 20½" pine (cabinet front)
E	1	¾ x 5 x 20½" pine (keyboard base)
F	2	¾ x 3⅝ x 4¼" pine (keyboard borders)
G	1	¾ x 5⅛ x 20½" (keyboard back)
H	1	¾ x 4⅜ x 20½" pine (internal baffle)
I	1	¾ x 7⅛ x 20½" pine (rocker support)
J	1	¾ x 8 x 20½" pine (music rack)
K	1	¾ x 5⅛ x 20½" pine (rocker cover)
L	1	¾ x 7¼ x 20½" pine (wind-chest top)
M	1	¾ x 4⅞ x 20½" pine (wind-chest front)
N	1	¾ x 6½ x 20½" pine (wind-chest bottom)
O	2	¾ x 4⅞ x 5¾" pine (wind-chest sides)
P_1	1	¾ x ¾ x 20½" pine (top cleat)
P_2	2	¾ x ¾ x 13¾" pine (cleats)
P_3	3	¾ x ¾ x 3" pine (cleats)
P_4	2	¾ x ¾ x 2¼" pine (cleats)
Q	1	½ x 1¼ x 20½" pine (music stop)
R	1	½ x 1½ x 13½" pine (key height adjuster) with four 1" No. 6 rh screws
S	25	½ x ⅞ x 2⅞" pine (rockers)
T	4	1½"-dia. pine (ball-shape handle supports)
U	2	½"-dia. x 11¼" hardwood dowels (handles)
V	60	⅜"-dia. screw hole plugs
W	75	1¼" No. 6 fh screws (cabinet screws)
X_1	8	¾ x ⅞ x 8" (white keys. Nos. 1,3,4,7,8,10,11,14)
X_2	2	¾ x ⅞ x 8" (white keys. Nos. 2,9)
X_3	4	¾ x ⅞ x 8" (white keys, Nos. 5,6,12,13)
X_4	1	¾ x ⅞ x 8" (white keys, No. 15)
Y	10	½ x 1⅛ x 5⅞" (black keys)
Z	25	¼"-dia. x 1" dowel (keyboard guide pins)
AA	25	¼"-dia. x 4" dowel (push rods)
BB	2	¼"-dia. x 15" steel rod threaded ¾" on both ends; four ¼-20 acorn nuts; four ¼-20 hex nuts; 24 felt washers (pivot rods)
CC	1	2 x 2" angle with two ½" No. 6 fh screws
DD_1	2	1½ x 1½" angles with four ½" No. 6 fh screws
DD_2	2	1½ x 1½" angles with four ½" No. 6 fh screws
EE	1	⅛ x ¼ x 13" self-stick foam weatherstrip
FF	25	¾" No. 6 rh screws (keyboard adjuster screws)
GG	25	¼"-dia. x 2½" dowel (rocker guide pins)
HH	50	7/16"-o.d. x 1" screw hooks
II	25	½-oz. egg-type fishing sinkers
JJ	25	1" No. 4 rh wood screws
KK		50-lb. test braided fishing line (50')
LL	25	No. 5 split shot fishing sinkers
MM	25	⅛"-o.d. nylon guide tube (at auto parts store)
NN	25	¾"-dia. x 3" dowel (air releases)
OO	25	¾ x ¾" sections of 1"-dia. PVC (for pipes Nos. 1 to 10); ¾ x ¾" sections of ¾"-dia. PVC (for pipes Nos. 11 to 25)
PP	25	½" No. 4 fh screws
QQ	25	⅛ x ¾ x ¾" felt
RR	25	½"-long screw eyes
SS	25	⅝ x ⅝" butt hinge; ⅝" brads (100)
TT	25	1½" safety pins
UU	as reqd.	Anodized aluminum tubing (organ pipes); 9' of 1" o.d.; 8' of ⅞" o.d.; 8' of ⅝" o.d.; 12' of ¾" o.d. See Pipe Chart for individual pipe sizes
VV_1	5	⅞"-dia. cone washers
VV_2	5	¾"-dia. cone washers
VV_3	9	⅜"-dia. faucet washers with ¾" No. 6 rh screws
VV_4	6	Size 00 faucet washers with ¾" No. 6 rh screws
VV_5	5	½"-dia. x 3½" dowel
VV_6	20	⅜"-dia. x 3½" dowel
WW	2	Cap-type hair dryers or equivalent
XX	2	¾" x 1"-dia. copper pipe reducers
YY	1	S.p.s.t. pushbutton switch; plug; 3 solderless connectors; lamp cord
ZZ		1/16" x 1-sq.-ft. felt

Misc.: Wood stain; varnish, silicone seal, white spray paint, black spray paint, contact cement, white glue, tape.

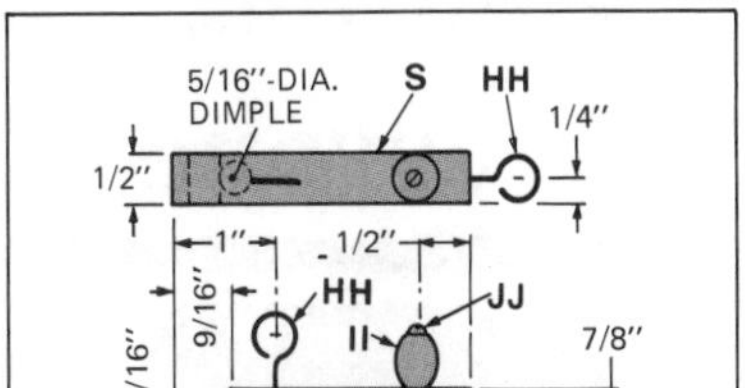
5/16"-DIA.
DIMPLE
S
HH
1/4"
1/2"
1"
1/2"
9/16"
HH
JJ
II
7/8"
5/16"
5/16"-DIA.
HOLE
5/16"
5/8"
2-7/8"
7/16"
ROCKER ASSEMBLY

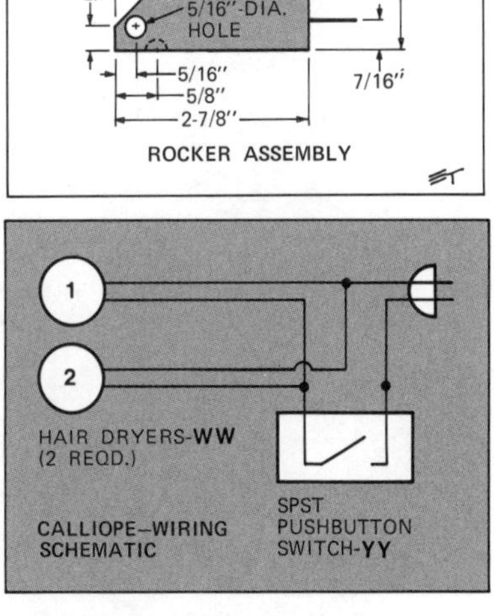
1
2
HAIR DRYERS-WW
(2 REQD.)
CALLIOPE-WIRING
SCHEMATIC
SPST
PUSHBUTTON
SWITCH-YY

THE KALEIDOSCOPE provides endless entertainment for a person of any age. A slight turn of the stained-glass wheels creates infinite variations of brilliant color, as shown by photos (below) taken through the tube.

Kaleidoscope that dazzles everyone

■ PUT THIS color-filled tube to your eye, and in seconds you'll see countless patterns of fiery red, sunny amber or icy blue. You can use up to 18 different colors and patterns of glass in the kaleidoscope. The greater the number of colors you use, the more vibrant the designs.

The kaleidoscope tube is a 1-ft. piece of plastic plumbing pipe (A) with an end cap (B). Bore the eyehole in the center of the cap and smooth the edges with fine (180-grit) sandpaper or steel wool.

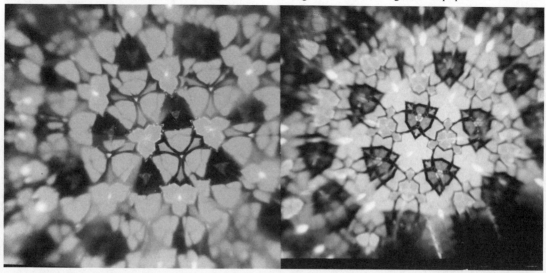

MATERIALS from top: 2-in. inside diameter plastic pipe and end cap, soldering iron, 50/50 solder, stained-glass scraps, copper spacers, bolt, washers, wood strips, wood block, mirror strips, acrylic circles, glazier pliers, pattern for stained-glass wheels, glass cutter and copper foil.

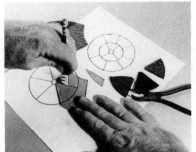

IF YOU CAN see through the glass, lay it on the pattern and score inside the inked lines with a sharp, oiled glass cutter. If the glass is too dark, cut a paper pattern for each piece and lay it on top of the glass so that it will act as cutting guide.

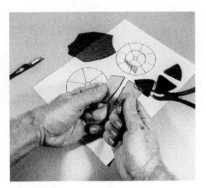

SNAP GLASS immediately after scoring it, using a downward and outward motion. Use pliers to break off small pieces. Rub edges of two pieces together to dull any sharp spots.

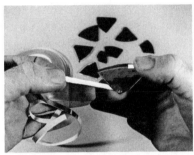

CAREFULLY center copper foil on edges of each piece of glass and wrap it tightly. Then smooth foil with dowel. Foil won't stick to greasy glass.

AFTER POSITIONING glass pieces on pattern and fluxing copper foil, run a bead of solder along edges, using a 60- to 100-watt iron. Then solder a piece of copper tubing in center as a spacer.

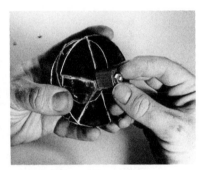

ASSEMBLE revolving unit; it consists of two glass wheels, acrylic disc, a wood block, bolt and nut.

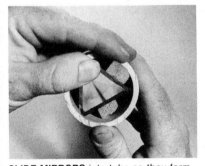

SLIDE MIRRORS into tube so they form a triangle, mirror side facing inward. Wood strips that hold mirrors should fit snugly, but be careful not to scrape any of the backing off the mirrors.

CEMENT end cap and acrylic eyepiece to one end of tube, and cement the glass assembly into the other end. Clean parts before assembly.

MATERIALS LIST—KALEIDOSCOPE

Key	No.	Size and description
A	1	2" i.d. (2⅜" o.d.) × 12" plastic plumbing pipe
B	1	2" i.d. plastic end cap
C	2	⅛ × 1⁹⁄₁₆ × 12" mirror
D	1	⅛ × 1¾ × 12" mirror
E	2	⅛ × 2⅜"-dia. clear-acrylic disc
F	2	½ × ¾ × 12" wood strip
G	1	½ × ¾ × 10½" wood strip
H	1	½ × ¾ × 1" wood block
I	2	¼ × ⅜"-dia. copper tube
J	1	No. 8-32 × 2" machine bolt
K	1	³⁄₁₆" i.d. nut
L	4	³⁄₁₆" i.d. washer

Misc.: 1 roll of ¼-in.-wide copper foil tape, 1 roll of 50/50 or 60/40 solid-core wire solder, 18 pieces of colored stained glass, glass cutter, pliers, oleic-acid flux, flux brush, cutting oil, 60 to 100-w. soldering iron, PVC solvent cement, epoxy resin cement, contact paper, inked wheel pattern.

Draw a full-size pattern of each color wheel on paper with a dark felt-tip pen. Lay a piece of stained glass over a section of one color wheel, with the smooth side of the glass facing up. Dip a sharp glass cutter into cutting oil or kerosene, then press the cutting wheel onto the glass along the inside of one of the inked lines. When you make the score, you should hear a slight hissing as the cutter travels over the glass, scratching a faint line into the surface. *Never* go over a scored line twice, however, or your cutter will quickly become dull.

If the glass you're using is so dark that you can't see the inked pattern through it, make a duplicate pattern on stiff paper. Cut out the pattern pieces and lay one on top of the glass to guide your cutter.

To make a quick break, form fists with both hands and grip the glass so your thumbs straddle the score line with fingers under the glass. Move your hands in a down-and-out motion to snap it.

Wash the glass with detergent and hot water, dry it, and then wrap copper foil around the edges of each piece so edges are centered on foil. Smooth foil with a dowel or pencil.

Lay the foil-wrapped glass on the pattern to check for fit. Then brush the copper with oleic-acid flux and solder the pieces together with 50/50 or 60/40 solid-core wire solder. Solder spacers (I) into the center of each wheel. Next cut the three mirror strips (C and D). Make the scores on the glass side, not on the silvered side. Then snap off the strips as you would any other glass.

Cut two clear-acrylic discs (E) to seal the ends of the tube. In one of the discs bore a ¼-in.-dia. hole with a center that is 7/16 in. from the edge. To secure the mirrors inside the tube, cut three wood strips (F and G) and wood block H. Bore a 5/16-in.-dia. hole through H.

Make sure all glass, mirror and acrylic parts are clean. Then cement the acrylic disc without the hole to one end of the tube. Slip end cap B in place. Slide the three mirror strips into the tube in a triangular shape, mirror sides facing inward. Carefully slide the wood strips in place. Position wood strip G under mirror D.

Slide the parts onto machine bolt J in the order shown above and secure nut K with epoxy resin. Apply epoxy resin to the open rim of the tube and to the wood block where it will be in contact with the tube. Position the wheel assembly and tape disc E in place until the epoxy hardens.

As a final touch, you might decorate the kaleidoscope with self-adhesive vinyl cut into simple shapes.

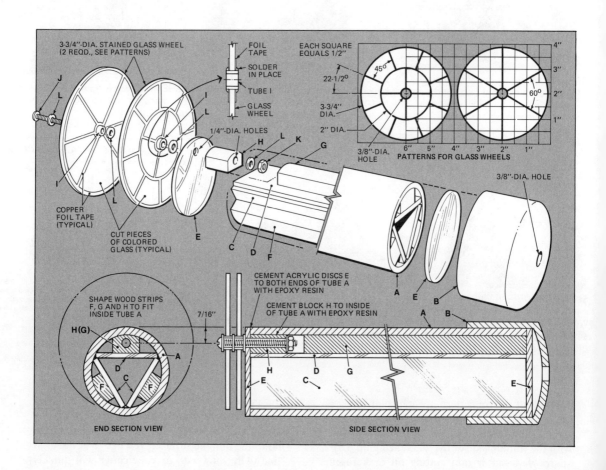

Fun projects

JEWELRY KEEPER

You can quickly build a surefire "corral" to keep small pieces of jewelry—earrings, pins, rings and the like—in one handy spot. The keeper shown is a project you can easily turn out in one day.

The "tree" at the back keeps the earrings in pairs; the clamp types on the crossbars, and those for pierced ears in the small drilled holes. Rings are neatly stacked on the short pole at the front, and pendants and pins can be stored in the scooped-out portion of the base.

You should use hardwood, such as walnut. The two posts and the dished-out section are turned on a lathe (the latter on the lathe faceplate).

Sand the turnings on the lathe, using a fine-grit sandpaper before making the cutoffs. Then assemble the stand, using glue, and let dry.

Finish with a coat of stain and wipe off the excess. Allow the keeper to dry for 24 hours, and apply wood paste filler. (This is necessary only if you are using an open-grain wood such as walnut, mahogany or oak.) Finally, spray on two coats of clear lacquer. After a two-week "curing," rub with double-0 steel wool and wax.

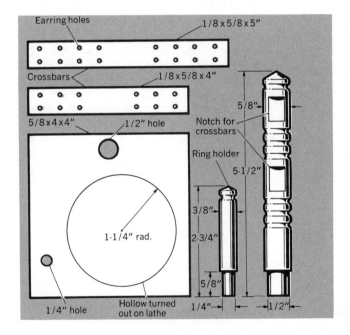

Earring holes   1/8 x 5/8 x 5"

Crossbars   1/8 x 5/8 x 4"

5/8 x 4 x 4"   1/2" hole

1-1/4" rad.

1/4" hole   Hollow turned out on lathe

5/8"

Notch for crossbars

Ring holder

5-1/2"

3/8"

2-3/4"

5/8"

1/4"   1/2"

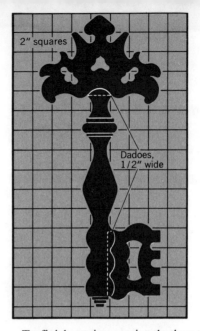

2" squares

Dadoes, 1/2" wide

KEY HOUSE NUMBER

A novel way to display your house number is with a replica of a keymaker's sign. It's easy to make, and when it's hung from the roof overhang, the early American touch enhances the look of the house.

The turned section is six glued-up 1x5s. While this piece is "square," cut the two ½-in.-wide dadoes for the handle and key sections. Then cut two blocks to fill the dadoes and glue them in place with water-soluble glue and use paper in the joint. Next, the turning is made. After completing the lathe work, the glued-in blocks can be easily pried out with a slight dampening and a chisel. Sand the turned section and set it aside. Now jigsaw the decorative handle and key sections and, after sanding the edges, glue these pieces in place on the turned section with waterproof glue.

The house numbers are jigsawed from ½-in. stock and are glued to a ¾-in. mounting strip fitted with screw eyes to accept the chain as shown. All parts are then assembled with a decorative chain. Though expensive, a solid brass chain is the best choice. But, if you prefer a less expensive chain, you can paint it with flat black enamel.

To finish, stain or paint the key to suit your home's exterior. If you prefer, the key can be antiqued (make distress marks with gouge, chisel or by beating with a chain). Since the key will be exposed to the weather, apply at least two coats of exterior varnish for maximum protection and long life.

A BAFFLING PUZZLE

Here's a puzzle that only you—and no one but you—will be able to solve unless you reveal its secret. Made as shown in the drawing, the smaller piece (with the dowel glued in) fits into the larger one. The object is to engage the notch in the rubber band which *appears* to be in the large piece.

The illusion that *you* can engage a rubber band is created by the way you withdraw the smaller part. To pull off the gag, you slide the plunger out an inch or so by gripping the tapered end between the thumb and forefinger. Then, when you squeeze, it will snap from your fingers and literally fly back into the block. Then, pass the puzzle to a challenger and sit back and watch as he finds it impossible to hook the band.

BAFFLING PUZZLE

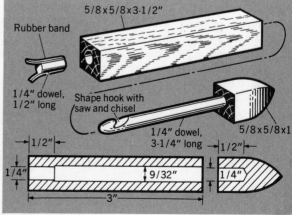

5/8 x 5/8 x 3-1/2"

Rubber band

1/4" dowel, 1/2" long

Shape hook with saw and chisel

1/4" dowel, 3-1/4" long

5/8 x 5/8 x 1

1/2"

1/4"

9/32"

1/2"

1/4"

3"

Little projects that take little time

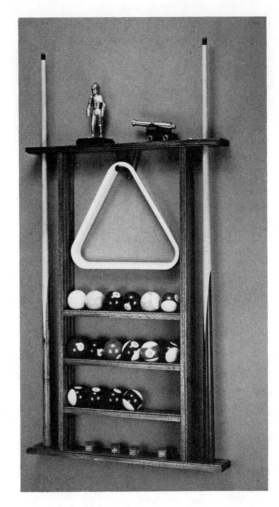

CUE-AND-BALL RACK

MODERN MAIL ORGANIZER

SWISS CHEESE MOUNTAIN GAME

SWISS-CHEESE MOUNTAIN GAME

In a race to scale this "Swiss-cheese" mountain, climbers on opposite sides must watch their step in maneuvering a table-tennis ball up the treacherous slopes. A slight miscue will send the ball through a hole in the "cheese" and back to the starting point. It's a game for two or four players (two to a team), and the climber (or team) who reaches the summit tray first wins.

Made in the shape of a wedge of cheese, the game consists of two ⅛-in. (or ¼-in.) hardboard sides that have 19 holes in them. Notice that the side holes are bored ¼-in. in from the edges and that no hole is more than ½ in. from each adjacent one. The section view shows how ramp

cleats, glued to the ¾-in. plywood ends, support a center partition and a sloping floor of ⅛-in. hardboard. A saw groove in the bottom of the summit tray fits over the partition so it is 1¼ in. down from the top.

To cut the slots for the dowels in the edges of the slanting plywood ends, set the saw fence a scant more than ½ in. from the blade. Then turn on the saw and carefully lower the work over the blade. Run the cut as far as you can, then stop and square it off with a hand or sabre saw. Hardboard strips cover the notches to hold the ½-in. dowel handles in place. Short sections of ¾-in. dowel cap the ends. The dowels should slide freely in the slots.

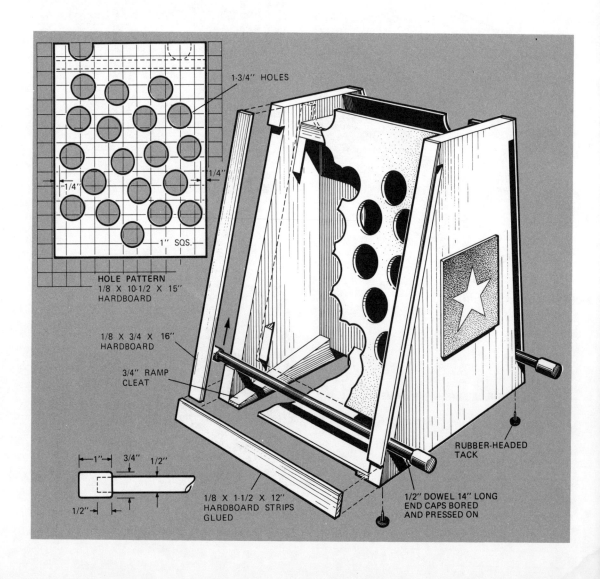

HOLE PATTERN
1/8 X 10-1/2 X 15"
HARDBOARD

1-3/4" HOLES

1/4"

1/4"

1" SQS.

1/8 X 3/4 X 16"
HARDBOARD

3/4" RAMP
CLEAT

1/8 X 1-1/2 X 12"
HARDBOARD STRIPS
GLUED

1/2" DOWEL 14" LONG
END CAPS BORED
AND PRESSED ON

RUBBER-HEADED
TACK

1" 3/4" 1/2"

1/2"

LL HOLES are bored in hardboard sides with a -in. hole cutter in a drill press.

MODERN MAIL ORGANIZER

In today's "paper world," almost everyone can use a mail organizer—the chief executive of the house, the homemaker, students and, of course, the office worker. For those of you in the final category, imagine the impression you'll make with this sleek IN and OUT box on your desk, especially if you paint it fireball fluorescent red.

Use ⅜-in. plywood to make it. Tacknail together the two side pieces and jigsaw or bandsaw both at once. Cut the three shelves, glue and nail the ends to them, then glue on the side panels. Sand a slight soft radius on all edges and corners. Set and putty the nailheads before painting.

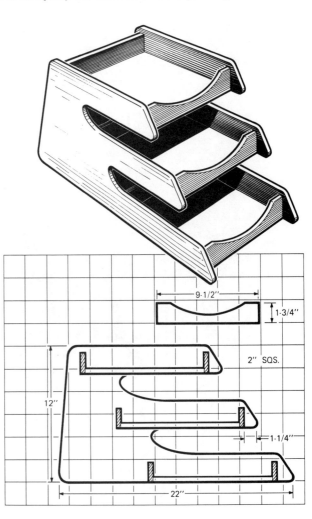

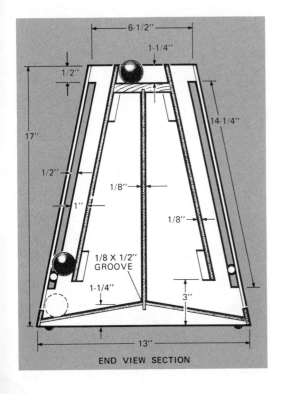

6-1/2"
1-1/4"
1/2"
17"
14-1/4"
1/2"
1/8"
1"
1/8"
1/8 X 1/2" GROOVE
1-1/4"
3"
13"

END VIEW SECTION

9-1/2"
1-3/4"
2" SQS.
12"
1-1/4"
22"

CUE-AND-BALL RACK

Rounding up the balls and cues when you're ready to "rack 'em up" is no problem when you store them in a handy wall rack. While this handsome one of walnut holds two cues, it can be built to hold four by making the outboard ends longer and boring extra holes top and bottom. Except for the size of the holes, the top and bottom pieces are alike, as are the sides and the three shelves. Make ball grooves in the shelves by passing the work diagonally across the blade of your table saw. Clamp a wood fence to the table and start with the blade only 1/16 in. high. Raise the blade 1/16 in. with each successive pass until you have a concave groove 1 in. wide. Hand-fin-ish the rough cut by wrapping sandpaper around a large dowel.

If you don't have a lathe, a length of dowel can be substituted for the turned rack peg. All parts are blind-doweled and glued together. Finishing is a lot easier if you do it before the rack is glued together. Apply strips of masking tape to the pieces at the glue joints to keep the wood free of stain. When the finishing is completed, peel off the tape and apply glue to the dowels. Glue and clamp the shelves to the sidepieces first, then add the top and bottom pieces and finally the peg bracket. Add two flat, metal hanging hooks to the rear edge at the top.

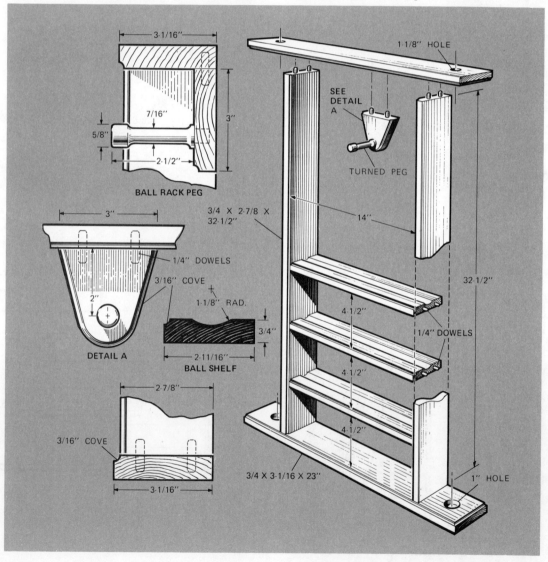

Music you can make in your shop

■ TUNED LIKE A DULCIMER and played like a banjo, a banjimer combines the sound qualities of both instruments. It's a joy to play and a great source of pride to the maker. Here is a project for the beginner or intermediate woodworker that is both challenging and fun to build. No two musical instruments are ever exactly alike. The drawing and materials list provide dimensions for an instrument of ideal construction in a technical sense. To make your instrument fit together well, you will have to adjust and fine-trim some of the dimensions.

Start construction by making the fret board. Choose a piece of clear, straight hardwood for the board. Lay out the positions of the frets and the nut by carefully following the measurements given in the drawing. This is one of the most crucial steps in the construction of the instrument. If any of the frets are in the wrong location, the notes will be off pitch.

Use guitar tuning pegs (called tuning machines by instrument builders). Buy the tuning machines (available in pairs) from an instrument repair shop. The dimensions of the peg box depend on the type of tuning machine you get, so buy a pair before doing more work on the fret board.

Use the machine to position ⅝-in.-dia. pilot holes for the slot and then bore them. Next, bore three holes in the edge of the peg box to accept the tuning machine. The holes in the edge are blind; they don't go all the way through the board. Use a coping saw to cut out the slot. Then cut the notch for the nut. The nut is a piece of

hard plastic about ¼ in. thick. Use a piece of scrap sheet acrylic or buy a guitar nut.

The frets are made of commercial fret wire. Fret wire has a T-shaped cross section with small barbs on the tail that extend into the wood. It requires no gluing, but the slot cut for it must be very thin. Use a coping saw or a very thin hacksaw blade to make the kerf.

Use a file and sandpaper to round over the rear edges of the fret board. Stop the rounded edge where the fret board will join the body, and just below the peg box.

Once all the woodworking operations are completed on the fret board, put the frets in place. Tap each fret in with a block of wood and a hammer. File the ends of the frets flush with the sides of the fret board and round them slightly so no rough edges catch your fingers.

Cut two ¼-in.-thick strips of plywood or prefinished paneling to form the cylindrical body. The two strips will be laminated together to form

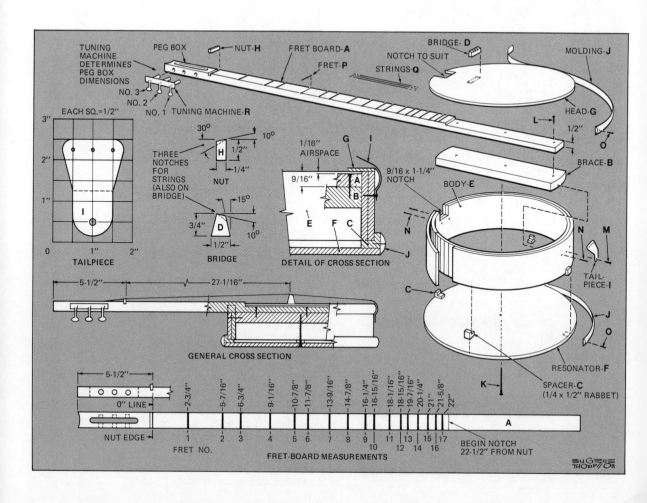

MARK POSITIONS of the frets and nut carefully, using a combination square. This is a most critical step.

TUNING MACHINES like one shown here have a rigid metallic construction. They must fit firmly into peg box.

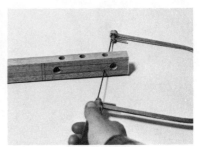

CUT THE SLOT in the peg box with a coping saw after you have finished boring the peg holes.

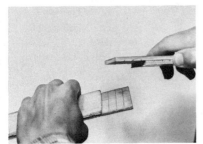

JOIN BODY PARTS as shown with half-lap joints and glue. Be sure that parts are cut to produce a fine fit before applying glue. Stagger the kerfs.

AFTER GLUE is applied to inner sides of body pieces, wrap body unit around a circular mold, such as a 10-in. pot. Secure with a web clamp or rope.

SCREW FRET BOARD to the brace. Nail the brace and glue it in place immediately after you have removed the body unit from its gluing mold.

a ½-in.-thick piece. Make saw kerfs across the width of the strips ½ in. apart and ⅛ in. deep to allow the body pieces to bend. Use a cylindrical object like a large pot with a 10-in. outside diameter as a mold and wrap the strips around it. Cut the strips to the exact length necessary to fit around the form and make a tight lap joint. Stagger the kerfs in the two strips to achieve maximum strength. Spread carpenter's glue evenly on the kerfed side of each strip and place the glued sides together; clamp the strips around the form with a web clamp or a rope twisted like a tourniquet.

When the glue is dry, remove the body from the mold and cut the notch for the fret board. Make the brace and install it inside the body with glue and four 1½-in. finishing nails; then, screw the fret board to the brace.

The head, or sound board, is made of ⅛-in. tempered hardboard. Cut the head slightly larger than the outside diameter of the body and cut a notch to fit over the section of the fret board that extends inside the body ring. Glue the head in place and clamp it securely. When the glue is dry, file the edges of the head flush with the sides of the body.

Prefinished vinyl molding (the type used in wall paneling) is used to cover the joint between body and head. Use contact cement to secure it in place. Put a small, prefinished paneling nail at each end of the molding for additional strength.

The resonator, or back of the instrument, is made of ¼-in. plywood or prefinished paneling. Cut it ½ in. larger in diameter than the diameter of the body and glue the four L-shaped blocks in place, as shown in the drawing. The rim around the resonator is also made of prefinished vinyl molding. Use contact cement and ½-in. brads to attach the molding to the resonator.

A penetrating oil finish is well suited for the fret board. If you used prefinished paneling for the body, no further finish is needed. If you used unfinished plywood, you can use a penetrating finish or varnish. Once the finish has been applied to the rest of the instrument, mask around the head and spray it with flat white paint.

When the finish has dried, install the strings. Start by installing the tuning machines. Then make the tailpiece from any type of sheet metal. Cut it out, using the pattern in the plans and attach it to the end of the banjimer with a round-head screw.

CLAMP A WOOD STOP to your miter saw for a ⅛-in.-deep kerf. Then use miterbox to make kerf cuts ½-in. apart.

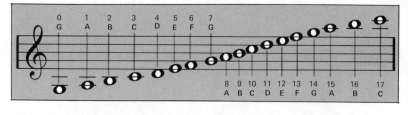

THE NOTES on the musical staff are identified above, along with the number which corresponds to the numbered fret on your banjimer. Use this key to play the melody for a few lines of the traditional folk song, "Red River Valley," below.

FROM	THIS	VAL-LEY	THEY	SAY	YOU	ARE	LEAV-ING.		WE	SHALL	MISS
4	7	9	9	9	9	8	9	8	7	4	7	9

YOUR	BRIGHT	EYES	AND	SWEET	SMILE.	FOR	THEY	SAY	YOU	ARE
7	9	11	10	9	8	11	10	9	9	8

TAK-ING	THE	SUN-SHINE,		THAT	HAS	BRIGHT-ENED	MY	PATH	FOR	A-WHILE.
7	8	9	11	10	5	5	4	7	8	9	8	8	7

USE PREFINISHED vinyl molding to cover the joint between the body and the head. Vinyl bends easily. Use a contact cement and small nail at each end.

The bridge is made of a hardwood (maple). Shape it to the cross section shown in the drawing. File notches in the nut and bridge for the strings. Use a triangular file and file the notches at an angle, so that the highest point of contact with the string will be closest to the playing surface of the fret board.

The three strings are No. 3 banjo strings. Run each string through a hole in the tailpiece until the end stops against the metal. If your strings have loop ends, install three small screws in the tailpiece for the loops.

The strings then pass through notches in the nut and the slot in the tuning peg. Turn each tuning peg to wrap each string around it. Once all the strings are installed, but not tightened, install the bridge. The bridge is not glued in place; it is held on by string tension alone.

The distance from the edge of the nut to the bridge must be exactly 27¹/₁₆ in.

Adjust the height of the nut and bridge by filing them until there is ¹/₃₂-in. clearance between

MATERIALS LIST—BANJIMER

Key	No.	Size and description (use)
A	1	¾ × 1¼ × 38¼" hardwood (fret board)
B	1	¾ × 2½ × 10" pine (brace)
C	4	½ × ½ × ¾" hardwood (spacer)
D	1	½ × ⅜ × 2" hardwood (bridge)
E	2	¼ × 2⅜ × 36" plywood or paneling (body)
F	1	¼ × 11½"-dia. plywood (resonator)
G	1	⅛ × 11"-dia. tempered hardwood (head)
H	1	¼ × ½ × 1¼" plastic (nut)
I	1	1½ × 2⅝" sheet metal (tailpiece)
J		¾" × 6' vinyl molding
K	1	2¼" No. 12 fh screw
L	3	1" No. 10 fh screw
M	1	½" No. 6 rh screw
N	4	1½" finishing nail
O	4	½" brad
P	1	Fret wire
Q	3	No. 3 banjo string
R	1	Tuning machine

Misc.: Carpenter's glue, flat white (spray) paint.

the strings and fret No. 1 and ⅛-in. clearance between the strings and fret No. 17.

Tune the melody string (No. 3) to any pleasing note, then fret that string at the fourth fret and match the drone strings (Nos. 1 and 2) to the pitch produced.

Pluck the strings with a guitar pick held in your right hand and fret the third string only.

Telephone installation

■ NOW THAT YOU CAN BUY AND IN-STALL your own telephone, how do you go about it? Here are answers to questions about phones and their installation.

Going modular

You can modernize your home to accept the new modular plug phones. The phone company and many electronics and department stores sell conversion covers for the standard type 42A terminal block. A converter consists of a new cover with a modular outlet and four color-coded snap-on clips. These are snapped onto the terminal screws in the back, according to color, and the conversion cover is tightened down.

The type 42A terminal block is the old type of baseboard connector to connect a telephone. When you take off the cover, you will see four terminals with four different color wires attached. The placement of these colored wires is crucial because they are the key to proper phone hookup. For many years, the phone system has used color coding as a way to simplify and speed installation. When you are installing any conversion device, you must match the colors of the wires to the proper terminals.

A modular plug is little more than a snap-in plug with four conductors in the tip. It mates with a connector inside a modular jack or converter. The telephone company made the change to the modular plug as a result of an FCC ruling that mandated standardization between the many phones on the market. The result is an easier plug to use.

You may find two different kinds of terminal blocks in your home: One type is a four-pronged jack, the other is a flush-mounted terminal block. It's easy to convert a four-pronged jack by using a modular converter. For the flush-mounted ter-

INSTALLING A MODULAR JACK

TO CONVERT a four-pronged jack to one that will be able to accept a modular plug, buy a modular converter. The modular plug from the telephone can then be plugged into the converter.

A TERMINAL BLOCK is found in some older homes. It must be replaced with a modular jack. Once replacement has been made, it's relatively easy to add your own phones.

TAKING THE TOP OFF the terminal block reveals color-coded wires. Carefully unscrew the terminals enough to loosen wires, and then remove unit from your baseboard or wall.

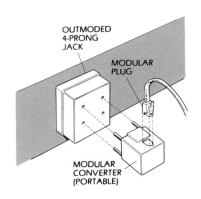

OUTMODED
4-PRONG
JACK

MODULAR
PLUG

MODULAR
CONVERTER
(PORTABLE)

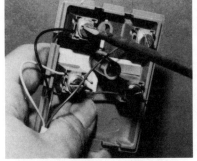

ATTACH THE MODULAR JACK'S BASE to the wall and then attach the wires in the same color-coded manner as before. Tighten screws and see that wires do not short against each other.

SNAP-FIT THE CONNECTIONS from the jack cover to the base terminals by simply following the color code. All you have to do next is to attach the jack cover, and you're finished with the job.

minal, you'll need a flush-mounted modular jack converter. Simply remove the old jack, leaving the wires hanging free, and then install the new bracket and snap-on clips. When this is done, insert and fasten the new modular jack and reinstall the faceplate.

Converting a wall phone outlet to modular involves removing the old phone by sliding it up and away and then removing the old base plate. When this is done, simply remove the old outlet, leaving the wires hanging. Next, install the new bracket and attach the wires to the converter plate by their color code. When this is done, tighten the converter into the bracket and attach the new base plate. Then slide the new wall phone over the clips.

The phone company supplies a modular plug converter to turn your nonmodular phone cable into a modular one. It requires that a four-wire cable be spliced according to instructions into the converter, which is then closed permanently.

Extending the wiring

When installing new, or extending existing, telephone wiring in your house, it's best to use color-coded, four-conductor wire, similar to what the phone company uses. This way, it's easy to be sure the wiring is correct. Running this wire behind the walls ensures maximum protection and prevents an unsightly tangle. Running it under a rug, on the other hand, means there's more chance for damage as people walk on it. Further, it can leave a ridge in the rug. Baseboard mounting is acceptable, provided you run the wire out of any potential walkways and it is secured to the baseboard with *insulated* staples.

Many phone companies install a network interface in homes. This is a tiny integrated circuit that protects the phone network from any harm by user-installed equipment. Older homes may simply have a terminal block instead of a network interface. Either is the demarcation point between the phone company's equipment and private home wiring. It's easy to install wiring beyond this point with a wire junction. Put this device near the interface, so they can be connected by the short modular plug cord attached to the wire junction.

ADDING A PHONE IS EASY if you use the right equipment. The portable, modular converter just plugs into one of the older-style, four-pronged jacks, and it can be moved from room to room. The permanent modular connector has four snap-on connections to attach to an existing base. Or you can install a completely new modular jack in place of your old four-pronged jack. Once you've gone modular, it's simple to connect extra wiring for extensions. The modular wire junction will plug into a modular jack and allow you to run two additional phone lines. Wall phones can be hung on just about any surface using special baseplates. And you can even get modular jacks with built-in covers that keep the dust out of the connection points.

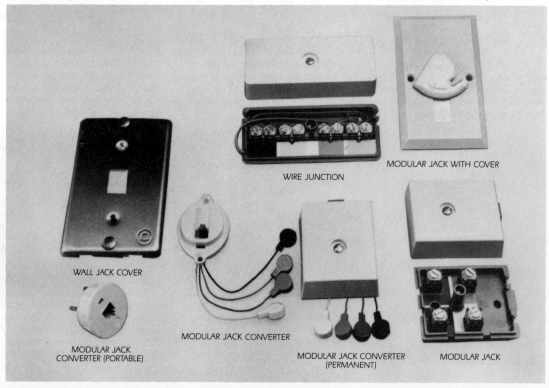

WIRE JUNCTION

MODULAR JACK WITH COVER

WALL JACK COVER

MODULAR JACK
CONVERTER (PORTABLE)

MODULAR JACK CONVERTER

MODULAR JACK CONVERTER
(PERMANENT)

MODULAR JACK

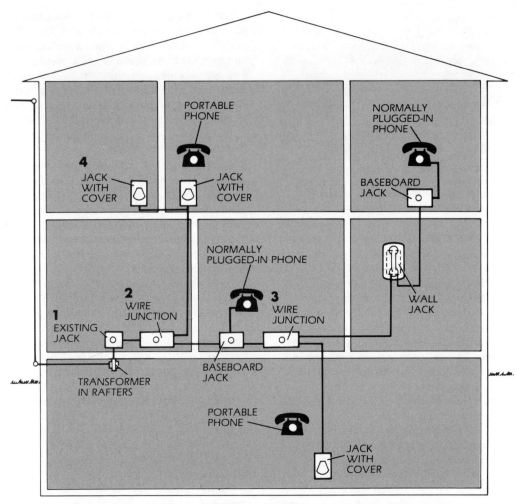

PORTABLE
PHONE

NORMALLY
PLUGGED-IN
PHONE

4
JACK
WITH
COVER

JACK
WITH
COVER

BASEBOARD
JACK

NORMALLY
PLUGGED-IN PHONE

2
WIRE
JUNCTION

3
WIRE
JUNCTION

1
EXISTING
JACK

WALL
JACK

BASEBOARD
JACK

TRANSFORMER
IN RAFTERS

PORTABLE
PHONE

JACK
WITH
COVER

HERE'S HOW to install extra extension telephone lines in your home. The incoming telephone line goes to the phone company's transformer and then to an existing jack or network interface [1]. At this point you may have to convert the jack to a modular one. Then connect a modular wire junction [2]. One line from the junction may connect to a new jack and from there to another junction [3]. The junctions simplify the wiring. Some jacks will have phones normally plugged in. Other jacks [4] may have a phone carried between them. These jacks should be the covered type.

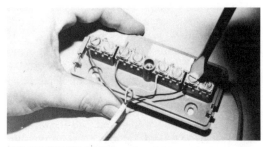

COLOR-CODED WIRES and matching colors on wire junction make it easy to install.

When this is done, determine the wiring paths for your home's new wiring, and then run this wiring to the areas where you are installing new phone outlets. After the wires are run, strip the outer covering off the ends of the cables to expose the four conductors inside. Install these thin wires in the wire junction according to their color coding. After you replace the cover, your house will be all wired for phones.

According to the American Telephone & Telegraph Co., the maximum distance you can run a wire from the network interface or junction box

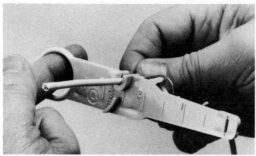

A WIRE STRIPPER TOOL is a handy device. The tool, with a built-in measuring scale, allows you to strip a multiconductor cable without damaging the wires. Afterward, you can use it for other wiring jobs.

is about 250 ft. This is the limit before line resistance and voltage loss become too great to run the phone.

There are some other precautions you should take. According to the phone company, a person installing a phone should be sure the installation complies with local building regulations and the National Electrical Code. Avoid placing telephone wires in pipes, conduits or compartments containing other electrical wiring. Never place telephone wiring near bare power wires or lightning rods, antennas, transformers, steam and hot water pipes, or heating ducts.

Before you fasten any wire to metal surfaces— siding, recreational vehicles or mobile homes— be sure no hazardous voltages are present on the siding or other conducting surfaces. And, you must never run wiring between structures where it may be exposed to lightning. Further, avoid damp locations or any place where wiring would allow a person to use a telephone while in a bathtub, shower or swimming pool.

Never use telephone wire to support objects. Be sure the wire is enclosed in electrical tape to protect it when it runs across gratings or other rough metal objects.

When drilling through walls or floors be careful to avoid contact with concealed pipes, other electrical wiring or similar items. You should also avoid running wire to temporary structures or to any locations not easily accessible, or anywhere the wire will be subject to mechanical stress or pinching, such as through door jambs or window sills.

Finally, keep the wire runs as short as possible to avoid interference with your phone system, and never splice one length of wire directly to another, because it can cause interference on your line. Instead, use wire junctions or modular jacks for multiple connections.

The phone company uses a system that supplies 48 volts and between 20 and 35 milliamperes of current. This provides excellent service on one phone. As you add extra phones to the line, you are dividing this current and voltage further, and the quality of the service deteriorates. Usually, no more than six to seven phones should be in a house and plugged in at once.

Buying your own phones

According to law, you must give the phone company (your local business office) the ringer equivalency number and FCC registration code of any new phone you buy to install. The ringer equivalency number indicates the type of ringer circuit in the phone. For operation of its lines, the phone company must know the type and number of phones you're using.

Some phone company systems use pulse dialing. This is a type of service associated with rotary phones. Inside a dial-type phone (called a rotary) there is a set of electromechanical contacts that turns the number dialed into a precisely timed sequence of electrical pulses. They are sent through the phone line to the central office, where they are decoded.

Sometimes a pushbutton phone can be used on a pulse system. If you have a unit from the phone company (any Bell-brand unit) it will work correctly. And, if you have a phone that has a pulse/DTMF switch it, too, will work correctly in the pulse mode.

DTMF stands for Dual-Tone, Multi-Frequency phone service. With it, two tones are generated every time the buttons are pushed. These tones are translated into electronic equivalents and sent through the system, where they are decoded at the phone company's central office. A rotary phone will work on such a system because the system still recognizes pulse dialing. You can mix dial and Touch-Tone phones in your home if you have this service.

With the wide variety of telephones available today, the choice of which type of phone to buy is up to you, but a phone capable of DTMF is best from a long-range reliability standpoint. Advanced-capability phones contain other features such as memory dialing, "hold," automatic dialing, redialing of a busy number and display of the time, date and cost of a call. The phone company also offers phones with features such as "speed" dialing a list of phone numbers, or services such as call-waiting and call-forwarding, but these are extra-cost options on your monthly bill.

Windows: an introduction

■ HIGH TECHNOLOGY WINDOWS made from space-age materials and with new energy-efficient glazings are changing the look of today's homes. Even traditional styles are now combined with vinyl or aluminum to make your home snug with units that always open without any strain.

The technological and efficiency developments in windows over the last decade are astounding. Modern windows look good, and operate and insulate far better than what was once available. Chances are very good that if your home has windows more than 20 years old, you may be considering replacement. This is a good time. The choices are many and the quality high.

WINDOW MATERIALS

It is interesting to look at the advancements in window manufacturing. In the 1940s, noninsulated (single-pane) wood windows easily dominated the market. In the 1950s, steel frame windows came on the scene. Still later, aluminum windows became available and captured a large share of both residential and commercial markets. In the 1970s, American window producers decided to follow the example of their European counterparts, which had been making and marketing vinyl-framed windows with great success since the 1950s.

Wooden windows

Wooden windows usually have jambs (including tops) the same width as the thickness of the wall from the siding through the face of the wall covering. The jambs are milled from standard 1-in. (nominal) boards, and the jamb liners are used to shim the window to fit the space. Sills also are included with the window package. They are cut from 2-in. (nominal) lumber and are pitched about 3 in 12 for water drainage. The sash are usually 1⅜ in. thick. Combination storm and screen units are 1⅛ in. thick.

Vinyl windows

Vinyl windows are available in a variety of colors and styles. Casement, single and double-

MODERN WINDOWS CAN ADAPT to any style. Here a traditional building has been refitted with long lasting, low maintenance, high efficiency insulated windows.

hung, picture windows, bay windows, bow windows, awning, hopper, slider windows and patio doors are all being used with greater frequency in both new construction or for replacement in older homes.

Solid vinyl windows have a number of advantages over wood and metal windows. These include the almost indestructible nature of rigid polyvinyl chloride (PVC) from which these windows are made. Wooden windows can rot, become stuck or difficult to operate and must be maintained by painting at least every 10 years. Aluminum windows tend to be cold, and the aluminum itself will corrode over time unless it has an anodized finish. Vinyl windows, however, are maintenance-free and can easily last as long as your house. Since the color of a vinyl window

VINYL WINDOWS never need to be painted, and will not swell, rust, rot or require regular maintenance. Vinyl is known for its high energy saving qualities.

goes throughout the material, scratches do not open part of the window to deterioration or color change.

TYPES OF WINDOWS

Types of standard windows readily available for do-it-yourselfers include double-hung, casement, fixed, horizontal sliding, awning and hopper, and jalousie.

Double-hung windows

Double-hung windows have two parts: an upper and lower sash. They may have a single

pane of glass or multiple panes of glass in each sash; the panes are called *lights*.

Double-hung windows provide more ventilation than any other type. One-half of the window may be opened. The windows are locked in window channels and move only up and down. One style has an easily removable sash for cleaning.

Double-hung window hardware, sometimes furnished by the window manufacturer, includes the sash lifts and window locks.

Casement windows

Casement windows are hinged along one edge and open out with a crank-and-gear mechanism or a single adjustable rod. Hardware usually is furnished by the manufacturer; it includes the crank and gear, hinges and sash locks.

Fixed windows

Fixed windows are large picture windows that don't open. Since they are usually glazed insulation glass, they don't need storm windows.

Horizontal sliding windows

Horizontal sliding windows are like standard double-hung windows that are tipped on their side. The sash move horizontally in guides or tracks. In multiple windows, several sash may be opened. In single units, one sash is fixed and the other is movable.

Awning and hopper windows

Awning and hopper windows are hinged at the top and open outward like an awning. A rod holds the window in different open positions. A hopper window is hinged at the bottom and opens outward at the top; it also has a rod that holds the window open. The jambs of these win-

STANDARD WINDOW TYPES are illustrated here. Metal frame windows also are available in many of these same styles.

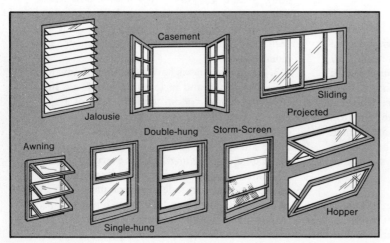

DOUBLE-HUNG WINDOWS on either side of a larger fixed window are used in this classic-styled bay window.

SLIDING WINDOWS

AWNING AND HOPPER WINDOWS

dows are usually at least 1 1/16 in. thick; the sill is at least 1 5/16 in. wide if multiple units are framed side by side.

Jalousie windows

Jalousie windows have a series of glass panels or slats that run horizontally across the window from its side frames. A crank-gear device opens and closes the panels. Wood-framed jalousie units are generally preferred over metal units because the insulation value of wood is greater than that of metal.

WINDOW CARE

Even if your existing windows are in reasonably sound condition, there are some things you can do to increase their overall efficiency—in-

AWNING WINDOWS are usually used in roofs, hinged at the top to open outward like an awning.

CASEMENT WINDOWS are hinged at the side and open with a crank-and-gear or a push-rod.

JALOUSIE WINDOWS have horizontal panes of glass that open together like blinds with a crank-gear device.

cluding an inspection of all windows to find loose or deteriorating putty, loose or broken window glass, old or nonexistent caulking, or a loose-fitting sash that allows warm air to leak from the house during the colder months.

Caulking windows

If you discover that the caulking around your windows and doors is old, cracked or missing, it is wise to apply new caulking before the heating season begins.

Oil-base caulks. On one end of the scale of the caulks available are the inexpensive oil-based caulks. These are generally not worth considering except where neither longevity nor appearance is a factor—such as the interior side of the foundation and sill plate joint in the basement.

Acrylic caulks. Acrylic, latex and butyl-based caulks are in the mid-range in price. These caulks are fine for applications where they will not be exposed to direct sunlight. Acrylic-based caulks are the most popular type and are easy to use.

Silicone caulks. Silicone-based caulks are considered the high end of all caulks and are probably the closest thing to an all-purpose caulk. Silicone caulks are expensive, and not always required. For example, if you are caulking a static, non-moving interior joint, almost any other type of caulking will be suitable. But if you never want to worry about caulking a joint again (either exterior or interior), then silicone-based caulking is the best choice.

How to caulk. When caulking around window and door frames you will get better results if you remove the old, deteriorated caulking first. This often takes time to do with a knife or paint scraper. It is also important to remove any loose paint, dirt and water. Even the best caulk will not adhere to a poorly prepared surface.

Once the joint has been cleaned thoroughly, apply a uniform bead of caulking. Although there are several schools of thought as to the best way to apply caulking, the most effective is to push the bead along the joint rather than pulling. By caulking in this manner, you can use the tube nozzle to both smooth the caulking and push it into the joint. Try to push the caulking gun along an entire joint in one smooth motion rather than in several motions.

After a joint has been caulked, it is often necessary to "tool" the new caulking. This is done to force some of the caulking into the joint and to give an even, concave appearance to the surface of the joint. Tooling can be done with a wet finger or, if you are using a silicone-based caulk,

with a wet plastic spoon, bowl side down. Special tools are also available for this final finishing of a caulked joint.

Within an hour, the average do-it-yourselfer can become an expert with a caulking gun. Of

CAULKING AROUND WINDOWS and doors will stop air leaks and make your home more energy efficient.

REPLACING OLD WINDOWS with modern windows is usually a simple matter.

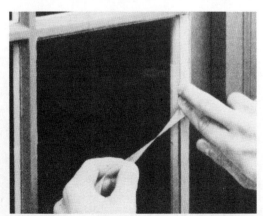

PRESHAPED CAULKING in easy-to-use rolls is applied by pressing in place, peel off the backing and then paint.

even greater importance, for the price of a few tubes of caulking you can increase the heat-holding efficiency of your windows and doors.

At least one manufacturer has found a way to take the pain out of glazing windows and caulking cracks with neat, easy-to-use caulk in pre-shaped rolls. Simply press the compound in place and peel off the protective backing. Then apply either a latex or oil-based paint.

Whichever type of caulking you choose for your sealing needs, read and follow the directions. Some caulks, such as silicone, produce irritating fumes during curing and can be toxic.

Loose-fitting sash

A common problem with older windows is a loose-fitting sash around the windows. This is often caused by a loose window guide or stop. To

MODERN WINDOWS are highly efficient and worthwhille investment for new construction or replacement.

solve this problem, you must remove the wooden window guides and renail them closer to the edge of the window frame. An acceptable guideline is to renail the window stop with a ¹⁄₁₆-in. space between it and the sliding window. In extreme cases, you will find it necessary to replace badly worn or deteriorated pieces of window stop to achieve a good seal around movable windows.

INSTALLING WINDOWS

Rough opening size (the actual size of the hole in the wall) varies with the style of window. If you know the exact dimensions of the rough opening, your dealer will tell you what window frame to buy and how much space there will be between the rough frame and window.

You should, however, allow 1¹⁄₁₆ in. to 1½ in. between the rough framing and the window for top, bottom and side jambs. This space will be

filled with shims to hold the window square and level in the opening.

HOW WINDOWS ARE SOLD

Windows are sold individually. If you order a number of windows, you may be able to get a discount from the retailer. The styles of windows that a retailer stocks may be limited, but you may be able to order a special kind if you know what you want.

Window hardware usually is included with the window units. If not, the hardware is sold as separate items. You can change the hardware included with optional period hardware or hardware that better suits your interior room design.

Window jambs and casings are sold by the linear foot. Some jambs come in kits priced as a unit rather than by individual pieces.

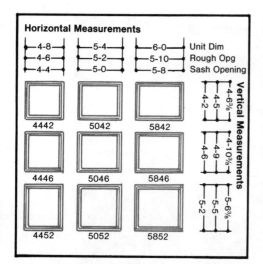

Horizontal Measurements

4-8	5-4	6-0	Unit Dim
4-6	5-2	5-10	Rough Opg
4-4	5-0	5-8	Sash Opening

4442   5042   5842

Vertical Measurements: 4-6³/₈ / 4-5 / 4-2

4446   5046   5846

Vertical Measurements: 4-10³/₈ / 4-9 / 4-6

4452   5052   5852

Vertical Measurements: 5-6³/₈ / 5-5 / 5-2

Unit Number	Dimensions of a 1-in. Glass Rabbet	Order this 1-in. Glass Size
4442	49 × 46½	48½ × 46
5042	57 × 46½	56½ × 48⅛
5842	65 × 46½	64½ × 46
4446	49 × 50½	48½ × 50
5046	57 × 50½	56½ × 50
5846	65 × 50½	64½ × 50
4452	49 × 58½	48½ × 58
5052	57 × 58½	56½ × 58⅛
5852	65 × 58½	64½ × 58

STANDARD PICTURE WINDOW DESIGNS are shown here. The horizontal dimensions of the windows are given directly above in the illustration, and the vertical dimensions are listed at the right. The unit numbers that identify each design are given under each window. Use these numbers when ordering. Compare the dimensions of your windows with the sizes shown here to find the exact size and the unit number to ask for. The chart lists the size of the pane of glass that fits each of these standard windows, assuming a 1-in. rabbet is provided all around the frame.

WINDOW SIZES are identified by four- or five-digit numbers, which the retailer uses in ordering. Here is a typical window schedule you can use for comparison and ordering. For example, the small window at top, left, number 20210, has the horizontal dimensions listed directly above, and the vertical dimensions listed to the right.

Glass Selection Guide

TYPE OF GLASS	RESISTANCE TO BREAKAGE	FOR D-I-Y INSTALLATION	COST
Standard single	Bad	Yes	Low
Standard double	Fair	Yes	Low
Tempered	Good	Yes	Medium
Plate	Fair	Yes	Medium
Safety	Good	Yes	High
Wire	Good	No	High
Insulation	Good	No	High
Blocks	Good	No	High
Tile	Bad	Yes	Medium

Note: Most paint and wallpaper stores stock these types of glass and cut pieces to order.

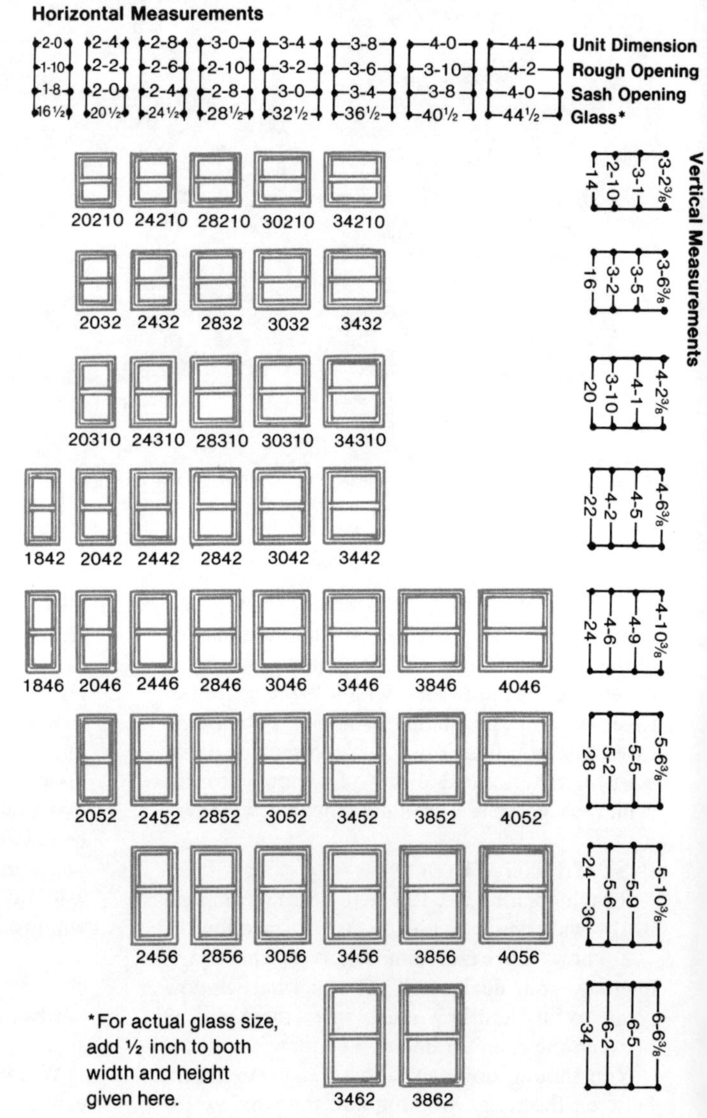

Horizontal Measurements

2-0	2-4	2-8	3-0	3-4	3-8	4-0	4-4	Unit Dimension
1-10	2-2	2-6	2-10	3-2	3-6	3-10	4-2	Rough Opening
1-8	2-0	2-4	2-8	3-0	3-4	3-8	4-0	Sash Opening
16½	20½	24½	28½	32½	36½	40½	44½	Glass*

20210   24210   28210   30210   34210

Vertical Measurements: 3-2³/₈ / 3-1 / 2-10 / 14

2032   2432   2832   3032   3432

Vertical Measurements: 3-6³/₈ / 3-5 / 3-2 / 16

20310   24310   28310   30310   34310

Vertical Measurements: 4-2³/₈ / 4-1 / 3-10 / 20

1842   2042   2442   2842   3042   3442

Vertical Measurements: 4-6³/₈ / 4-5 / 4-2 / 22

1846   2046   2446   2846   3046   3446   3846   4046

Vertical Measurements: 4-10³/₈ / 4-9 / 4-6 / 24

2052   2452   2852   3052   3452   3852   4052

Vertical Measurements: 5-6³/₈ / 5-5 / 5-2 / 28

2456   2856   3056   3456   3856   4056

Vertical Measurements: 5-10³/₈ / 5-9 / 5-6 / 24 / 36

*For actual glass size, add ½ inch to both width and height given here.

3462   3862

Vertical Measurements: 6-6³/₈ / 6-5 / 6-2 / 34

Roof and casement window installation

■ REPLACING AN OLD WINDOW with a new one or adding a new window where there wasn't one before are two of the most popular home remodeling jobs. In the first case, you can often boost your home's energy efficiency—and in the process lower your heating bills. In the second case, you can transform a poorly lit room into one much more pleasant for living and working.

In most cases, window installation is the kind of job that a homeowner will "contract out" because the task seems too imposing. Actually, it's very straightforward and well within the abilities of those who are willing to install new roof shingles and siding, fix-up a front porch or even build an exterior deck on the back of their house.

Following are step-by-step instructions for installing an operable roof window and a standard two-pane casement window. The roof window shown here was new installation; the casement was a replacement job. But both can be installed either way, depending on your requirements.

Roof window

To start with, remember that a roof window is not what is commonly called a "skylight." Although both are installed in similar places and both do let in a great deal of extra light, the roof window has an operable sash instead of fixed glazing like a skylight. This permits the roof window to act as a ventilator in the summer, especially when installed in attic rooms.

Begin by determining where you want the window to be. The manufacturer recommends that this window be placed low enough to afford a good view when seated. But other positions are just as viable depending on the structure of your house and privacy considerations. The best way to choose the position is to cut out a section of cardboard to match the window you want to buy and hold it against the ceiling in various places until you are satisfied. Then, trace the cardboard shape on the ceiling and remove the ceiling to expose the rafter cavities. The ceiling here was

MADE OF WOOD and completely flashed with aluminum, the roof window (above) can transform a poorly lit attic room into a desirable work area. Sash operates by pulling handle latch (right).

covered with painted knotty pine boards that we carefully removed to use later.

Once a few rafters are exposed, you may want to alter the position of the window slightly to save cutting a rafter or two, depending on the width of your window.

Next, determine how you want to trim the window after it's installed, because this will dictate where you must place the window header and rough sill. We chose what the manufacturer called a "horizontal soffit lining with a vertical sill lining." The results are shown clearly in the photos. This arrangement does yield the greatest light penetration, but the window can also be trimmed so the jambs are perpendicular to the sash on all sides.

CHOOSE WINDOW LOCATION inside room, then remove ceiling—in this case, pine boards—to expose rafter cavities. Measure across rafters to relocate window position.

BORE HOLE through roof at centerpoint of desired window position. Then, slide dowel or piece of scrap wood into hole to act as measuring reference point on top of roof.

POSITION ROOF BRACKETS below area to be cut using dowel as reference. Attach by lifting up tabs and nailing directly to roof. Then, lay sturdy plank across brackets.

HOOK TAPE on dowel to locate window, then draw rectangle on roof. Use a framing square for accuracy and check measurements from corners to eaves and ridge.

REMOVE SHINGLES from interior of rectangle, then cut through roof sheathing using carbide blade in circular saw. Set blade depth so cut is just below bottom of sheathing.

PRY OFF SHEATHING BOARDS—or plywood sections, depending on roof— using flat bar or wrecking bar. Be sure to remove all nails from boards and rafters before proceeding.

Next, locate the centerpoint of the rough opening and bore a hole through the roof at this point. Push a wood dowel or piece of scrap wood into this hole to act as a reference point for measuring the opening outside.

Move to the outside and install the roof brackets and plank as shown. These brackets— and the reciprocating saw used for cutting the rafters—are common rental items. Nail the top of these brackets directly to the roof underneath a shingle tab to avoid damaging the roof. When the brackets are removed, it's a good idea to fill the holes with a few dabs of plastic roof cement and press the tabs back down into it.

Once the brackets and plank are installed, lay out the rough window opening on the roof. Measure from the dowel centerpoint and draw the rectangle using a framing square and chalkline so the outline shows up well on the roofing. Also, measure from the eaves and ridge to the corners of the rectangle to make sure the top and bottom of the opening will be parallel to the ridge and the eaves. It is extremely important that the opening be square and to the exact size given in the manufacturer's instructions.

Next, remove the shingles from the interior of the outline and put them aside for filling in later. Then, make the cuts as shown using a circular saw with a carbide blade set to a depth that just cuts through the sheathing. Remove the boards or plywood from the cut and immediately remove all nails in both the sheathing and the rafters as a safety precaution.

Now, go inside and frame a wall section to use as a temporary brace when cutting out the rafters. Use 2 × 4 stock, with studs on 16-in. centers, and drive the wall into place underneath the ceiling just above the opening you plan to cut. If this wall fits snugly, you don't have to nail it into the floor or ceiling.

Begin marking the rafters to be cut by establishing a plumb line on the surface of the rafters that form the corners of the opening. Then establish the sill and header positions, relative to these lines, following the maker's instructions. Make the cuts, starting at the sill end followed by the header end. Install the double 2 × 6 header and sill using 16d common nails.

Complete the rough opening by installing the short rafter—or rafters—between the header and sill so they align with the edge of the cut sheathing above. Check for precise square before nailing these in place.

Next, remove the sash from the window frame following the manufacturer's instructions. Pay particular attention to how the sash is removed because reinstalling it later—at least on this window—can be tricky. Then, mount the frame into

BUILD A TEMPORARY BRACING WALL using 2 × 4 stock, then drive it under ceiling above rafters that will be cut. If fit is tight, wall does not have to be nailed in place.

PLACE LEVEL against edge of sheathing and draw plumb line across surface of rafter. Do the same on rafter at other side of opening, then snap chalkline between both points.

LOCATE INSIDE SURFACE of window header, then measure up 3 in. along rafter and make parallel mark, perpendicular to rafter edge. Cut this line using reciprocating saw.

WINDOW HEADER is made of two 2 × 6s nailed into ends of cut rafters and toe nailed into sides of uncut rafters. Nail first 2 × 6 in place, then nail second one into first.

ROUGH WINDOW SILL is framed like header above with doubled-up 2 × 6s. Nail first 2 × 6 into ends of cut rafters and sides of uncut rafters. Then, nail second into first.

TOE NAIL a short rafter between the header and sill, so its bottom edge aligns flush with both. The rafter's inside surface should fall just below edge of cut sheathing.

REMOVE SASH from frame, then attach L-shaped hanging brackets to frame sides. Lift frame onto roof, center in opening, then screw brackets into roof sheathing.

SURROUND FRAME with overlapping pieces of roofing felt. Start at bottom, followed by sides and top. Curl up felt against frame and keep nails 8 in. from opening.

USE OLD SHINGLES to fill in roofing around frame. Start at bottom and work up, alternating shingles with L-shaped step-flashing to make window weatherproof.

the opening. On this unit, L-shaped steel brackets are mounted on the frame sides first, and then the frame is screwed directly to the roof as shown. Because this roof had two layers of shingles in place, we removed the new ones about 18 in. around the opening and installed the brackets on top of the old shingles. This maintained the proper projection of the frame above the roof so the flashing would fit right.

Next, cover the sides of the frame with roofing felt as shown, then flash the unit according to the instructions. This unit came with aluminum step flashing that was alternated with every shingle as we moved up the roof. This unit also has an aluminum cap piece that covers all the jambs and the step flashing below. After the frame is in place, install the sash from below, then trim the interior.

Casement window

The most effective way to deal with old, drafty windows is to simply replace them. There's no better long-term solution and windows are available in a wide variety of styles and sizes which make replacement straightforward.

The basic steps in replacing a window are: First, determine the rough opening of the old window. If necessary, remove the window's interior trim molding to measure the opening. Next, order a replacement window that is equal to or slightly smaller than the old window. Making the opening slightly smaller is much easier than enlarging it to accommodate an oversized window. Then, remove the old window, modify the opening, if necessary, and install the new window. And

remember, there's no substitute for quality, so purchase the best window you can afford. Any money saved with low-quality windows will probably be lost to higher heating bills. Always be sure that you check the local building code before starting any construction.

To illustrate the procedures involved, we replaced a 28-year-old single-pane metal casement window with a new vinyl-clad wood casement window equipped with double-pane insulating glass. The left side, as viewed from the outside, opens for ventilation and cleaning. Casement windows also come with righthand vents and both left- and righthand vents in one unit.

The first step in taking out the old window is to remove the exterior house siding or shingles from around the window. Take off only as much material as is necessary to uncover the window trim. Using a hammer and a wood block carefully pound along the *inside* window jamb to loosen the unit from the house. Now move outside and use a pry bar to pull the window free.

Next, modify the rough opening dimensions, if necessary, to accept the new window. For the installation shown, the opening width and height had to be decreased slightly to yield the rough opening that was recommended by the manufacturer.

Now, nail wood strips of the same thickness as the sheathing around the face of the opening. Cut the strips wide enough to bring the sheathing flush with the inside edge of the rough opening. Next, staple wide strips of 15-pound roofing felt around the exterior of the opening. The felt helps prevent air and water infiltration.

AFTER LOOSENING THE OLD WINDOW from the inside, move outside and pull the unit from the house using a pry bar. This casement window was nailed through the exterior casing.

PRY OUT THE WINDOW TOP first. Grip window frame and pull the unit from house. Keep window closed to make the unit more rigid.

FRAME-IN THE ROUGH OPENING ff necessary, to accept the new window. Nail stock to the header first, then to sides, as shown.

NAIL STOCK TO THE HOUSE to bring the sheathing flush with the opening. Use material that is the same thickness as the sheathing.

STAPLE 15-POUND ROOFING FELT around the rough opening before stallation to deter air and water penetration.

PLACE THE NEW WINDOW into the rough opening, bottom first. Keep pressure against the sill while positioning the top.

PLUMB THE WINDOW, then nail through the holes in the vinyl anchoring flange. Use large-head galvanized or aluminum nails.

Now place the new window in the opening from the outside. While you hold the window, have a helper check the window for plumb. Add wood shims where they are necessary. Then, nail through the prebored holes in the window's vinyl anchoring flange using large-head galvanized or aluminum nails. Be careful not to strike the vinyl flange or it may crack, especially during very cold weather.

Next, replace the house siding so that it over-laps the vinyl anchoring flange and then caulk around the window. Now you should move inside to finish the window interior.

Since wall thicknesses vary, most windows come with extension jambs that allow you to build out the window flush to the finished interior wall. Extension jambs are available in a variety of wid-ths to accommodate most walls. If it is necessary, rip the extension jambs to fit flush to the wall. Then, nail the extension jambs in place and fill the spaces around the window with fiberglass insula-tion. Be sure you don't pack the insulation in too tightly or its insulating value will be greatly re-duced. Now, install casing molding and finish the interior woodwork as desired.

HOW TO HANG DOUBLE-HUNG WINDOWS

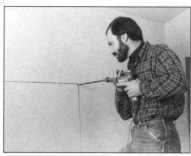

TRANSFER THE ROUGH OPENING LOCATION to the outside wall by boring through the wall with a long electrician's drill bit.

SNAP CHALKLINES from hole to hole to outline the window's rough opening. Then, use a circular saw to cut out the sheathing.

MEASURE 1½ IN. below the opening and make a deep plunge cut at each stud to establish the position of the sill plate.

SINCE A CIRCULAR SAW can't cut through the stud entirely, use a reciprocating saw to cut the remaining ½ to ¾ in. of wood.

AFTER SAWING through the studs at the sill and header locations, move inside and cut out the plasterboard using a compass saw.

BREAK AWAY the plasterboard and hammer the studs free. If you remove more than two studs, be sure that you brace the ceiling.

DRIVE THE WINDOW header into the wall above the rough opening. Build the header from two 2x6s with a ½-in. spacer between.

INSTALL THE WINDOW from the outside and secure it by nailing through the vinyl anchoring flange. Then, you can replace the shingles.

Basement windows

Frame and finish a basement window

A common problem is encountered by many homeowners when remodeling a basement: How to frame and finish a window that is recessed back from the foundation wall. The answer: Install an extension window jamb made of 1 x 6 or 1 x 8 No. 2 pine ripped to the appropriate width.

First, frame out a rough opening around each window with 2 x 3s. Cut the header and sill 2 in. longer than the window width. Nail the header 1 in. above the window opening and the sill 1 in. below the window.

Next, determine the width of the jamb. Measure the distance from the window frame to the *finished* wall, then rip the pine stock accordingly.

Cut and assemble the jamb so its inside dimensions clear the window opening by at least ¼ in. on all sides. Assemble the jamb using 2-in. finishing nails and butt-joined corners. Next, hold the jamb in the rough window opening and use cedar shingles to shim it into position. Be certain the bottom of the jamb is level with the window opening and that the jamb sides align with the window frame.

Check the jamb for square and then drive 2½-in. casing nails through the jamb and shims and partially into the 2 x 3 framing. Once again, check the jamb for square before driving the nails all the way in. Then, toenail the back of the jamb into the window frame using 1½-in. finishing nails. Apply caulking where the jamb meets the frame.

Finish the wall with plasterboard or paneling. The finished wall should be flush with the jamb. Finally, trim the window opening with casing molding. Paint the jamb and trim as desired.

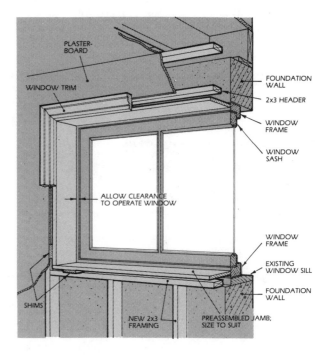

WINDOW TRIM
PLASTER-BOARD
FOUNDATION WALL
2x3 HEADER
WINDOW FRAME
WINDOW SASH
ALLOW CLEARANCE TO OPERATE WINDOW
WINDOW FRAME
EXISTING WINDOW SILL
FOUNDATION WALL
SHIMS
NEW 2x3 FRAMING
PREASSEMBLED JAMB; SIZE TO SUIT

WHILE FRAMING out the basement walls, build a rough opening around the window that is at least 2 in. larger on all sides.

PREASSEMBLE THE JAMB before you nail it into the rough opening. Use 2-in. finishing nails and butt joints.

USE SHIMS to hold the jamb in position for nailing. Be sure to check the jamb for square before you drive in the nails.

Reglaze windows

Replacing a broken pane of glass is a relatively straightforward task, but it can be dangerous. To begin with, always wear tough work gloves when handling the broken shards and the new glass. Also, because the glass is installed on the exterior side of the window, it's best to remove the sash and make the repair on a bench.

The steps shown apply to wood frame windows. On older metal frames the procedure is basically the same, but spring clips instead of glazier's points are used to secure the glass. If you have a newer aluminum sash, replacement usually involves a rubber or plastic retaining gasket, not glazing compound. For all types, cut the glass ⅛ in. shorter—in both dimensions—than the opening.

IF THE COMPOUND IS TOO HARD to chip away easily, use a hair dryer or flameless heat gun to soften it first. Be careful not to char the sash when using the heat gun.

ONCE THE BULK of the compound and all the glass have been removed, use a paint scraper to clean the muntin and frame rabbets. For best results scrape down to bare wood.

APPLY A LIGHT COAT of linseed oil to the bare wood so it will not absorb oil in the fresh compound. Otherwise, new compound will dry, lose flexibility and crack sooner.

SCORE GLASS in one quick stroke using a glass cutter and metal square. Butt glass and square to stop board as shown, and lubricate cut line with touch of kerosene.

MOVE SCORE LINE over the edge of the cutting surface and snap the glass with a quick downward motion. Wear gloves when handling the glass to prevent cuts.

APPLY A ⅛-IN. BEAD of compound across all rabbets to form a tight interior seal and to act as a cushion. Lay the glass in place; press evenly into compound.

SECURE GLASS with glazier's points pushed into the muntin and sash frame every 4 in. The push-type points shown are much easier to use than the flat triangular points.

ROLL FRESH COMPOUND between your hands to form an approximate ⅜-in.-dia. "rope." Lay the rope into the corner formed by the glass and frame, then press it into place.

DRAW A FLEXIBLE PUTTY KNIFE over compound to form a neat bevel. Allow compound to dry one week before painting, then let paint overlap glass ⅛ in. for a good seal.

Broken window pane replacement

■ SOONER OR LATER most homeowners can count on having to replace a shattered window pane. Knowing how to loosen the old putty, bed the new glass, hold it with glazier's points and strike a neat bevel when applying the putty seal will save you the frustrating job of trying to get someone to come and fix it. A propane torch and caulking gun make the job go faster, but they are not essential. If you work carefully, you can remove the old putty with a sharp chisel, and you can apply the putty by hand without a gun. A hammer and a putty knife are the only other tools you'll need.

The easiest way to get a replacement pane is to take the dimensions to a hardware store or a glass dealer and have the pane cut to fit. Allow 1/16-in. clearance all around so the pane will slip easily into place with no binding.

Variety of thicknesses

Glass comes in various thicknesses. *Single-weight* window glass is 3/32-in. thick; it is normally safe to use in sizes up to 2x2 ft. *Double-weight* window glass is 1/8-in. thick; it is normally safe for use in sizes up to 3x5 ft. *Heavyweight* glass is 7/32-

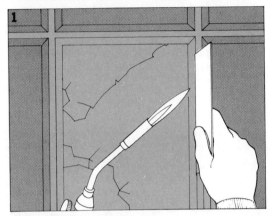

HEATING OLD PUTTY with the flame of a torch softens it, makes it easier to remove. Avoid scorching the wood by using a shield of scrap tin.

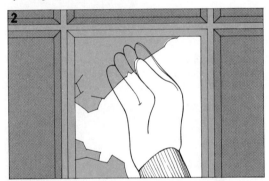

SAFE WAY to remove a cracked pane is to cover it with strips of masking tape and crack further with a hammer. Wear a glove when pulling out broken pieces.

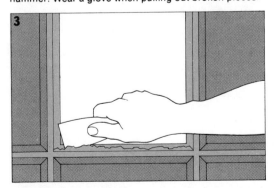

SCRAPE PUTTY CLEAN from rabbet with a knife or chisel, pry out old glazier's points and brush rabbet clean. Seal bare wood with thinned oil-base paint.

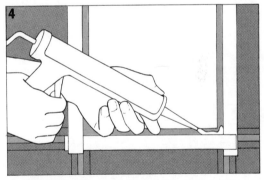

SILICONE RUBBER sealant or regular putty can be used to bed the glass. If silicone is used, outline the opening with tape to keep off adjacent panes.

PRESS NEW PANE (with 1/16 in. allowance on all sides) in place until sealant oozes around edges for tight seal. Remove excess with putty knife.

in. thick and is recommended where high gusty winds or other hazards may occur. Even heavier glass is available from glass dealers for table and countertops, large sliding doors and other specialized uses.

How to set the window pane

Run a bead of putty or silicone rubber all the way around the rabbet for the pane. Then press the new glass into place, applying equal pressure on all sides. Continue to press until the putty or sealant oozes all the way around the pane.

Next, drive glazier's points into the wood trim to hold the pane in place. You'll find a small driving tool packaged with the points. On a small pane use one point on each of the short sides of glass, two points on the long sides. For larger panes, use your own judgment.

Roll a ribbon of putty between your hands and string it along one side of the pane. Dip your putty knife into turpentine, then form a neat bevel in the putty.

Let the putty dry for several days, then paint it to improve the appearance and keep the putty from shrinking away from the glass and the wood trim.

It is easier to clean the window of putty marks after the putty has hardened for a few days.

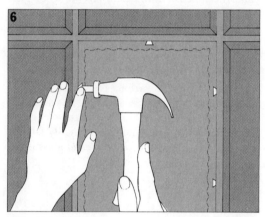

DRIVE GLAZIER'S points, size 1 or 2, using driving tool packaged with points. On small pane use one point along the short sides of glass, two on long sides.

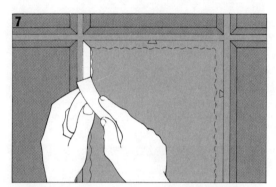

FOR FINAL BEVEL, silicone or putty is smoothed with putty knife dipped in solvent or turpentine to keep material from sticking to the knife blade.

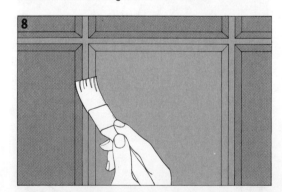

IF PUTTY is used, it should be painted several days later when it's dry. Painting the new putty improves appearance and keeps it from shrinking.

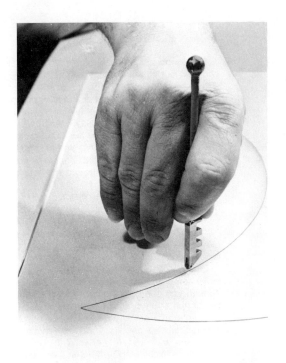

TRACING a contoured pattern on glass is possible if the cutter is kept well oiled and sharp.

TWO BASIC TOOLS—plate pliers and a glass cutter—were the only ones used to complete this quarter-moon design in glass. For such work, the benchtop must be covered with a scrap piece of short-pile rug.

Glass cutting short course

■ MOST OF US have lived through at least one exasperating work session in which a couple of sheets of glass were shattered by clumsy glass-cutting efforts. Usually, the aggravation is compounded later when you stand in the glazier's shop and watch him make the cuts while hardly looking at the material. With the tips listed here, plus the right tools and some careful practice, you should come close to duplicating his expertise.

A good glass cutter can be purchased at your hardware store. If you plan to do any pattern cutting, you'll also need plate pliers. For most work, straight pliers—with the jaws ground *so the tips meet first*—will suffice. The only other tools needed are tape measure, straightedge and a square. Finally, your worktable cutting surface should be covered with a piece of short-pile rug.

When making a straight cut on either sheet or plate glass, similar techniques are used, but

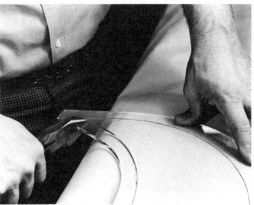

THE PATTERN to be cut from glass is traced onto paper. The paper is placed under glass and the glass scored, following the pattern. After the excess glass is removed, the score line is "run" (above) with plate pliers.

there is a slight variation in cutter pressure. As a rule, sheet glass requires roughly twice the pressure that plate glass does due to its harder surface. Never apply excessive pressure because the glass will fracture on the surface, and the cut will run erratically.

Because of the cutting wheel's shape, a straightedge should be placed $1/16$ in. away from and parallel to the intended cut. Before scoring, dip the cutter wheel in a lightweight motor oil.

Score with one movement—no stops. The cut should sound smooth and be free of skips. After scoring, the cut can be run (removed). If the cutoff is 1 in. or less, remove it with plate pliers. Let the glass hang over the cutting-surface edge. Then place the flat end of the pliers on the score line and apply a downward twist to peel off the glass in one piece. If the cutoff piece is more than 1 in. wide, the glass can be snapped off.

In pattern cutting, place the paper pattern under the glass. With cutter in normal position, follow the pattern on the glass. Before breaking, remove all excess material to within 1 in. of the score line, then run the original cut.

ABOUT GLASS

Contemporary glass terminology isn't complicated, but you may still hear some outdated expressions. The term "plate" is still sometimes used to suggest quality, but true, ground and polished plate glass is no longer made. "Sheet glass," too, is virtually extinct. Nearly all flat glass is now made by the float process. A wide belt of soft but solidifying glass is pulled across a pool of molten metal. Often such glass is even flatter than the old ground and polished plate was.

This annealed float glass has strength proportional to its thickness. Hardware stores usually stock common window thicknesses. For thicker glass—for a big picture window, for example—go to a glass shop instead of a hardware store.

Since a glass cutter is a seldom-used tool, make some practice cuts on scrap if possible. Though you can hold the cutter as if it were a pencil and apply pressure with your index finger, most pros prefer the more stable grip between first and second finger shown below. Here, the ball end of cutter rests on your knuckles and, by placing the first finger on top and your thumb directly underneath—and the notches facing down—you will be able to master this handy—but sometimes ornery—tool.

Making straight cuts

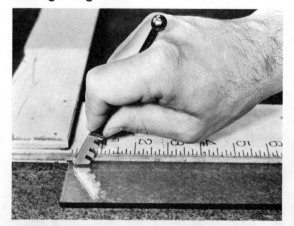

A PROPER GRIP on the cutter is important when moving it along a straightedge. The grip shown above is the best method. A small strip of glass (top right) is snapped by placing the flat edge of the pliers on the score line and applying a downward twist. To break off a large piece (right) the straightedge is carefully placed squarely under the score, then the glass is snapped off by applying a quick, definite pressure. Notice that all glass-cutting steps are done on carpet to avoid breakage by impact.

Wine rack has a handy tray

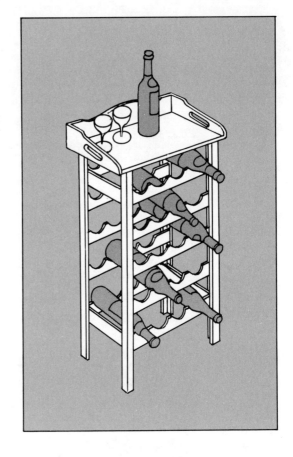

■ FEATURING a lift-off tray, this wine rack makes serving wine extra convenient.

Use a fly cutter to cut the bottle notches. Break the hole edges with a corner-rounding router bit, sand with a 3-in. drum, then rip the boards.

First, preassemble two rail units (upper and lower) using glue and finishing nails to form two rectangles. Then attach them to the front posts with glue and one diagonally driven screw. Next, drill screw pilot holes through the backs of the three front rails, and glue and screw. Finally, glue on rear posts and attach the rails to the legs with screws driven from the backs.

SET FLY CUTTER for 3½-in. hole. Clamp work to a scrap board and drill-press table (above). After cutting holes, rip the board to produce half-round notches (below). Or holes can be cut with sabre saw.

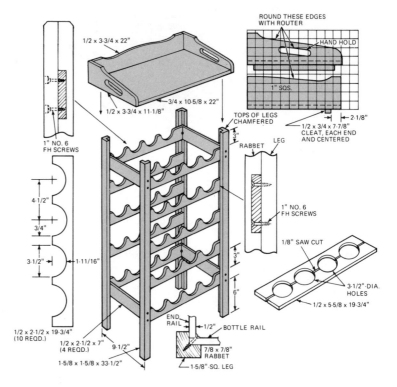

ROUND THESE EDGES WITH ROUTER

HAND HOLD

1" SQS.

TOPS OF LEGS CHAMFERED

RABBET

LEG

1/2 x 3/4 x 7-7/8" CLEAT, EACH END AND CENTERED

2-1/8"

1/2 x 3-3/4 x 22"

3/4 x 10-5/8 x 22"

1/2 x 3-3/4 x 11-1/8"

1" NO. 6 FH SCREWS

4-1/2"

3/4"

3-1/2"

1-11/16"

3"

1" NO. 6 FH SCREWS

1/8" SAW CUT

3"

6"

3-1/2"-DIA. HOLES

1/2 x 5-5/8 x 19-3/4"

1/2 x 2-1/2 x 19-3/4" (10 REQD.)

1/2 x 2-1/2 x 7" (4 REQD.)

9-1/2"

1-5/8 x 1-5/8 x 33-1/2"

END RAIL

1/2"

BOTTLE RAIL

7/8 x 7/8" RABBET

1-5/8"-SQ. LEG

1 OUR OAK RACK interlocks and joins together without hardware; each box holds six bottles of your favorite wine. Reproduction bin pulls add a hint of mission furniture to the handsome rack.

Wine racks you can build

■ IT'S SAFE TO SAY that many people who buy wine by the case like to display their stock as part of their home decor. On these pages, we show three wine racks created in our workshop. Plans and instructions for making all three are on the following pages.

The racks shown on these pages satisfy various needs: No. 1 is a clever box-type arrangement that can be used one atop the other, as shown, or individually, if preferred. The sides, top and bottom interlock in an ingenious system. No. 2 is for those who stock considerable amounts of wine. You might never guess it with a quick glance, but there are more than four cases of wine bottles in the pair of large racks shown in the photograph. No. 3 is a traditional Mediterranean-style iron wine rack. Each circular bay is used to contain one bottle; the rack holds 18 bottles in all.

THE OAK RACK

This countertop beauty is designed using the modular system. Each module holds six wine bottles, so you will need a pair if you buy your wine by the case. The tops and bottoms of the module sides are routed to a specific rabbet conformation, and the top and bottom pieces are dadoed to receive the sides.

The result is a rack that stacks securely without any hardware. If you desire, the top can be removed by lifting off.

Start by cutting the parts to size. Since you are working with oak, make certain you work only with sharp blades and cutting tools. After cutting all the parts, sand them smooth, starting with 100-grit paper and finishing with 120.

Cut the rabbets in the side pieces before assembly. Lay them out as shown in the drawing and use your router and a ⅜-in. rabbet cutter. Because you are shaping oak, you should make the cuts in two passes. Do the first pass at half-depth and the final one at full depth. The rabbet width must be at least half the thickness of the wood stock.

When the cuts are completed, sand the sides, using 150-grit paper to remove any "whiskers" that have been made by the router cutter.

Assembling the modules

Next, assemble the modules. You install the bottle racks using blind dowels and white glue. Use a minimum amount of glue to avoid squeeze-out. If any glue should squeeze out of a joint, allow it to dry and harden overnight. The next day, you can remove it cleanly and easily, using a razor-sharp chisel.

The easiest method for assembly is to use the techniques shown in the photos. Make sure you use match marks on the rack ends and mating surfaces of the sides so the module will go together without aggravation.

When it is assembled, clamp the module and allow it to stand overnight; use protective scraps of wood or cardboard between the clamp jaws and the wood to protect from tool marks.

2 THIS WINE RACK has the capacity to hold all of your prize stock—about 10 cases. Crafted in plywood, the rack gets its strength from interlocking diagonals. The natural finish gives it a clean look.

3. SPANISH-STYLE ornamental iron rack is an excellent project for those who prefer to work in metal. The rack shown holds 18 bottles.

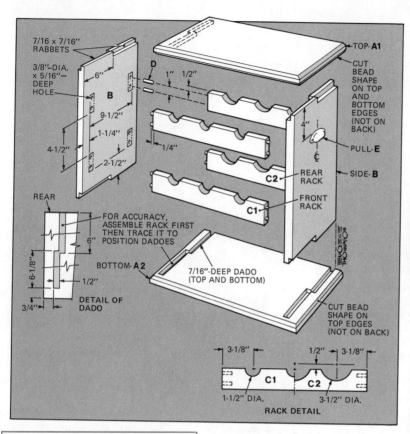

7/16 x 7/16" RABBETS

3/8"-DIA. x 5/16"-DEEP HOLE

TOP-**A1**

CUT BEAD SHAPE ON TOP AND BOTTOM EDGES (NOT ON BACK)

6"

B

9-1/2"

1-1/4"

4-1/2"

2-1/2"

D

1"   1/2"

1/4"

PULL-**E**

4"

C2

REAR RACK

SIDE-**B**

FRONT RACK

C1

REAR

FOR ACCURACY, ASSEMBLE RACK FIRST THEN TRACE IT TO POSITION DADOES

6"

6-1/8"

1/2"

3/4"

DETAIL OF DADO

BOTTOM-**A2**

7/16"-DEEP DADO (TOP AND BOTTOM)

CUT BEAD SHAPE ON TOP EDGES (NOT ON BACK)

THOMPSON

3-1/8"   1/2"   3-1/8"

C1   **C2**

1-1/2" DIA.   3-1/2" DIA.

RACK DETAIL

MATERIALS LIST—OAK RACK

Key	No.	Size and description (use)
A	2	⅞ x 12¾ x 18½" oak (top and bottom)
B	2	⅞ x 12 x 14⅝" oak (sides)
C	4	⅞ x 2 x 15¼" oak (front and rear racks)

Key	No.	Size and description (use)
D	16	⅜"-dia. x 1¼" hardwood dowels
E	2	Brass pulls

Misc.: 100-, 150-, and 180-grit sandpaper; oak stain; tack cloth; semigloss varnish; turpentine.

THE INTERLOCK FEATURE

1 To create the interlocking joint, use the router freehand or to a stop.

5 To prevent chance of router drift, clamp on a guide for the shoe.

9 Use dowel centers to transfer marks from racks to sides. Note the marks.

Cut the top and bottom pieces to size and shape the edges using your router. Next, align the module on the base piece.

The rack should be flush at the back and the space at the ends should be equal. Check these dimensions and move the module about until they are correct.

Using the router

When you're satisfied with the rack position, trace around both rabbeted ends, using a pencil. Remove the rack and set up the base piece for routing with a straight cutter. Make a test cut in scrap to check the dado for width and depth. Also, stop the router in the scrap and mark the outermost edge of the shoe on the scrap. Remove the router and measure the distance from the mark to the cutter edge.

Use this dimension to locate the fence (guide) for your router to ride against when routing the dadoes in the bottom (and top). Remember that you will only cut halfway across, and then the guide must be moved ⅜ in. to finish the other half of the dado. Clean out the rounded corners, using a sharp narrow chisel. Make certain you test-fit the mating members frequently as you do this dado-shaping step.

Repeat the procedure to create the top piece. Make certain that you mark the top, using the *top ends of the module.* Remember that there is almost always some warp or cup in a piece of hardwood; thus, it is very likely that your rack top and bottom pieces will only stack one way—the way they were laid out originally.

Finishing the rack

When all carpentry is completed, you can proceed with the finish. *Note:* You can rout the rab-

2 Avoid damage to wood by making the first pass at half-depth.

3 Clean out the rounded corners left by the bit, using a sharp, ¼-in.-wide chisel.

4 After box is assembled, position it on base, mark for dadoes. Repeat for top.

6 Carefully clean out dadoes using a chisel.

7 To avoid drill-bit drift in end grain, center-punch holes.

8 Bore dowel holes to desired depth; note masking-tape depth stop on bit.

10 Bore blind dowel holes on marked sides. Check the drill stop often.

11 Cut dowels to length, apply glue and insert them into the rack.

12 Align match marks, assemble rack. Use at least four clamps overnight.

bets in the sides freehand if you are experienced with a router. If you have reason to doubt your control of the tool, clamp a stop block to keep you from routing beyond the rabbet center point.

Sand the entire rack with 150-grit paper, dust or vacuum off the sawdust and apply the oil stain of your choice. The rack shown was stained with Spanish oak oil stain. Apply the stain, following label instructions. After wiping the piece, let it dry for 24 hours.

The rack shown is sealed with 3-lb.-cut, water-white shellac thinned 50 percent with denatured alcohol. Use a quality bristle brush to apply it and allow the shellac to dry for at least four hours.

To finish, lightly rub the shellac with 180-grit paper wrapped around a felt block. Rub lightly, and with the grain only. Dust off the piece and wipe thoroughly with a tack cloth. Apply one coat of varnish, as it comes from the can. The rack shown was finished with semigloss varnish, which dries to a "hand-rubbed waxed" look.

EGG-CRATE RACK

Intended for serious wine buffs, this pair of racks holds about five cases each, for a total storage space of 10 cases. Like the oak rack, it is built using the modular system. In the photo we have two racks arranged to display a modest wine collection.

This rack is made with ½-in. birch veneer plywood. All exposed plywood edges are faced with ⅛-in.-thick strips of solid birch. The angled joining blocks are cut from ⁵⁄₄ stock. If you can't obtain solid birch in this size, you can substitute maple because it has a fairly similar appearance.

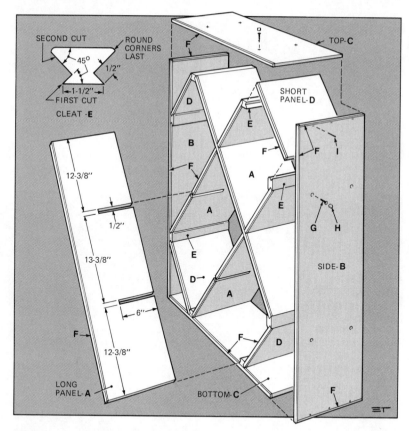

1 Use a block plane to trim edge banding flush with panel surface, then sand.

5 Masking tape must be used to hold glued joint together; clamps won't hold.

Start by sawing the panels to size, making sure to allow for the add-on ⅛-in. strips. You won't need clamps to glue on the strips; use masking tape instead to apply the necessary gluing pressure. Cut the strips ⅝-in. wide to permit some leeway in gluing. They are trimmed flush to the panel surfaces with a block plane after the glue has set. Don't skimp with the tape; use 6-in.-long strips at 3-in. intervals to obtain good contact throughout. A word of caution about masking tape: Some brands of tape leave a sticky residue when removed; this type must be avoided. Test the tape on scrap to make sure yours comes away clean.

Notching the cross panels

The diagonal cross panels are assembled with edge half-lap joints: ½-in.-wide notches are cut halfway through the mating pieces. You can make these notches in one pass on the radial-arm (or table) saw, using a dado head. If you don't have a dado head, simply make two kerf cuts with a smooth-cutting, regular saw blade.

Here's how to obtain uniformly spaced cuts:

Clamp a stop on the radial-arm fence 12⅜ in. from the blade. Cut 6 in. into the panel to make the first cut for a notch, then flip the panel over, *end-to-end,* and make the first cut for the second notch. Do this with the eight panels, then shift the stop block so the second kerf cut will be ½ in. from the first one, measured outside to outside.

Don't automatically shift the block ½ in. from the first position, or you will have an error equal to the saw blade thickness! Repeat the sawing on the eight panels, alternately flipping them over for the second notch cut.

A quick way to drop out the notch waste is to bore a ½-in.-dia. hole at the inside juncture. Otherwise, use a sabre saw with a narrow blade and work it across the corner. Sand the faces of all the panels. This tends to loosen the fit of the panels in the notches, but the slight looseness is okay. In fact, a tight fit will cause assembly problems.

Making the joining blocks

Now, you make the angled joining blocks. These can be made on either a table or a radial-arm saw. Here's how it's done on the table saw:

2 Make double kerf cuts to form notches. Do all first cuts, then shift.

3 Two 45° bevel cuts are first made on lower part of the joining blocks.

4 Fence is repositioned and the blade is elevated for the second cuts.

6 Test-fit panels together; do this work on a flat surface for accuracy.

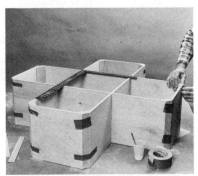

7 To obtain tight joints when gluing in end panels, hold them with duct tape.

MATERIALS LIST—EGG-CRATE RACK		
Key	**No.**	**Size and description (use)**
A	4	½ x 11⅝ x 39⅛″ birch plywood (long panel)
B	2	½ x 11⅝ x 38¾″ birch plywood (side)
C	2	½ x 11⅝ x 38″ birch plywood (top, bottom)
D	4	½ x 11⅝ x 12⅛″ birch plywood (short panel)
E	8	1⁵⁄₁₆ x 2½ x 11¾″ birch (cleat)
F	36 ft.	⅛ x ½″ birch (edging)
G	16	1½″ No. 8 fh screw
H	16	⅜″-dia. dowel plug
I		6d finishing nails (as reqd.)

Tilt the blade for a 45° bevel cut. Make two passes in each block to cut the shallower bottom kerfs first. Then raise the blade and reposition the fence to make the second series of cuts, which will drop out the waste. These deeper cuts are made last so *a nontippable wide surface is always on the table.*

If you should have a molding cutter head for the saw, with a suitable small-radius shape, use it to cut the small corner-round on the blocks. Otherwise, do the rounding over with a block plane and sander. Sand all of the exposed surfaces of the blocks before assembly.

The blocks are glued to the panel ends for the first stage of assembly. Here, masking tape is an absolute necessity because ordinary clamps simply can't get a proper hold. Two strips of tape pulled taut will suffice. To make sure you join the blocks to the correct faces of the panels, join the panels in advance and mark the block locations. One slip-up will mess you up.

How to interlock panels

After the glue has set, interlock the panels (they won't need glue), then cut the smaller end panels to length. Working on a flat work surface,

glue them in place. Since many plywood panels have some degree of warp, it is advisable to use a stronger tape for this gluing operation to ensure against the parts popping apart. Duct tape is a good choice. Again, check the product first for clean sticking and removal.

Wood screws and glue are used to attach the side members. The heads are then concealed with wood plugs. Clamp the top and bottom members in place and bore ¹⁄₁₆-in. pilot holes for the screws. Remove the clamps, bore the shallow larger hole for the plug, then rebore for the screw body and shank diameters, respectively. Glue and screw the top and bottom panels in, repeat the steps and attach the left and right side members. The abutted corners are secured with glue and 1½-in. (4d) finishing nails. When both sections are completed, stack them one atop the other and drill the screw holes for the mending plates. These plates will serve to keep the sections from shifting.

Finishing the rack

If you have paint spray equipment and a suitable place to work, you can apply practically any

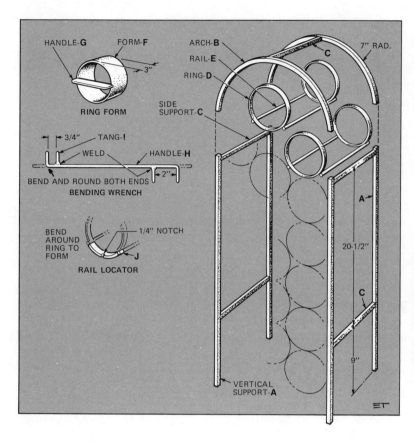

HANDLE-G FORM-F ARCH-B RAIL-E RING-D 7" RAD.

RING FORM

C

SIDE SUPPORT-C

3/4" TANG-I
WELD HANDLE-H
BEND AND ROUND BOTH ENDS 2"
BENDING WRENCH

BEND AROUND RING TO FORM 1/4" NOTCH
J
RAIL LOCATOR

A

20-1/2"

C

9"

VERTICAL SUPPORT-A

1 Form the rings around the ring form. Hold form in a vise.

5 To bend the main arch, insert the steel between tangs of the wrench.

kind of finish. But brush application of a regular top-coat finish will be particularly difficult in those angled corners. A good solution is to use a penetrating Danish oil finish.

MEDITERRANEAN WINE RACK

A solid furniture accessory, this metal wine rack is 36 in. high, weighs 35 pounds and holds 18 bottles of wine. Each bottle is held within two rings, one at the neck and one at its base. A number of blacksmithing and welding techniques are utilized in its construction.

Begin by shaping the rings. If you have a power hacksaw, you can slice ½-in.-thick sections of a 5- or 6-in.-dia., thick-wall pipe.

An alternative method, shown here, is to make a form around which to bend the rings (see the ring-form detail in the drawing). A section of 5-in.-dia., thick-wall pipe can serve as the form. Weld a strip of steel across the bottom of the form to secure it in a vise.

Using the bending wrench

A bending wrench shown in the drawing helps

shape the rings. One other shopmade tool, a rail locator (see detail J), is used later to locate the rails supporting the wine bottles. Since it has the same contour as the rings, shape it when you bend them.

Use a hacksaw to cut the strips for the 36 rings to length. Grind all ends smooth if needed. Secure the form in a vise. Lock one end to the form with lever-jaw pliers and bend the ring by pulling and bending with the bending wrench. Close the rings with a C-clamp and weld the inner and outer surfaces together. Grind the weld clean. True up the ring in a vise with a hammer. The main arches of the wine rack are 14 in. in diameter. One way to shape them is to use an automobile wheel as a form. Heat the length of ½-in. square steel in a forge or with an oxyacetylene torch to cherry red.

To avoid heating the steel, you can also bend the arches, using a vise and the bending wrench. First lay out the arch shape on cardboard. Then secure the bending wrench in the vise, tangs upward. Place one end of the steel between the tangs and begin to bend; continue bending the

2 The C-clamp keeps the ends of the ring together while they are welded.

3 Clean the outside of the ring weld on a bench grinder. Hold ring vertically.

4 Clean hard-to-reach spots with a small portable grinder.

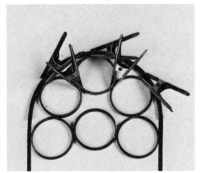

6 Clamp first three rings to arch and to each other. Weld parts together.

7 Clamp rails to 2x4s to hold securely while they are being welded.

MATERIALS LIST—METAL RACK

Key	No.	Size and description (use)
A	4	½ x ½ x 30″ mild steel (vertical support)
B	2	½ x ½ x 22″ mild steel (arch)
C	5	½ x ½ x 12″ mild steel (side support)
D	36	$\frac{3}{16}$ x ½ x 15¾″ mild steel (ring)
E	36	¼″-dia. x 12½″ mild steel (rail)
F	1	3″ x 5″-dia. thick-wall steel pipe (ring form)
G	1	$\frac{3}{16}$ x 1½ x 5″ boiler plate (ring-form handle)
H	1	⅝ x ⅝ x 15″ mild steel (wrench handle)
I	2	⅝ x ⅝ x 1½″ mild steel (wrench tang)
J	1	$\frac{3}{16}$ x ½ x 2½″ mild steel (rail locator)

length of the steel, occasionally removing the work and checking the shape against the arch.

After bending both arches, check to see that grind smooth the ends that will rest on the floor. Weld supports to the arches.

Next, position the three top rings within one of the arches; test-position the rest of the rings, then remove them. Clamp the first three rings to the arch and to each other and weld them in place. Clamp and weld the remaining rings. Attach rings on the second arch to line up with their mates; clean welds. Join arches by welding the side supports. To keep arches plumb and square,

clamp several flat pieces of steel bridging the 12-in. gap between arches.

To find the position of the rails that hold the bottles, first find the exact bottom of each ring. You can do this by placing a piece of shot, a dried pea or a pencil inside each ring and marking the spot where it settles. Line up the notch of the rail locator with this mark; mark the ring at each end of the locator. Turn the rack upside down and weld a rail onto the bottom of the ring directly above these two outer marks.

Finish by spray painting black with a rust-resistant metal paint.

Ski care

■ YOU CAN DAMAGE even the toughest pair of skis, no matter what they're made of and no matter what the salesman says. Even the best equipment, worn by a downhill expert or touring novice skier, is subject to scraping, crossing, bottom gouging, edge dulling and burring. If you believe the "maintenance-free" stories, you're going to shorten the life of your equipment. And at a steep price tag for some of today's top-design FRP (fiberglass-reinforced plastic) "schusslat-

zen" for instance, you'll be throwing away money if you skip the simple preventive maintenance that keeps skis going in winter and safely stored off season.

Proper waxing: hot or cold

Proper waxing tops your checklist. Waxing comes after the edges have been sharpened (since fillings can become embedded in paraffin) and can be done hot or cold. Satisfactory cold methods include the old rub-on stick wax technique as well as more modern paste and spray treatments. Cold waxing is easy and convenient, especially for touch-ups on the slopes, and should be done a couple of times during the ski day, often matching wax type to snow conditions.

Hot wax coats, applied by iron-on or paint-on methods, last longer. An iron at medium heat is held, point down, over ski bottoms and wax

SKIING PERFORMANCE can be affected by the condition your skiis are in. Check and wax your ski bottoms periodically. Also, be sure to sharpen your edges regularly.

pressed against it until the wax melts and can be dribbled down one side of the ski, outside the groove, and up the other. Ribbons of wax are ironed out evenly over the entire surface—keep the iron moving so the base won't loosen its bond with the ski. Afterward you'll have to buy a new iron, of course.

Transporting skis safely

Waxing keeps polyethylene bases from wearing down quickly, prevents oxidation, helps turning by avoiding tip-scrape. Tops of skis can use car wax to help guard against road salt when skis are carried on exterior racks. Almost as much minor damage can happen while toting equipment as during actual use. Off the rack, skis should be carried bottom to bottom and strapped together to prevent edge scissoring. Transporting them inside the car is dangerous to skis and riders in case of a sudden stop. When using a public carrier, box your gear or use a ski bag. Wrap newspapers between skis to avoid marring waxes' bases. Bagged in canvas, burlap or plastic on a roof rack, skis are protected from flying debris.

Storing skis

Store skis vertically in wood racks at ski areas and at home so snow can drain off and no one will trip over them. When finished for a weekend—or season—wipe skis dry, wax tops and bottoms lightly and coat edges with light oil or petroleum jelly. Modern skis don't need to be blocked in the middle to maintain camber, but should be stored away from temperature extremes. Strap together and suspend from cellar beams or closet hooks. Wall racks from ski stores are good. Rest ski tails on wood blocks rather than concrete floors.

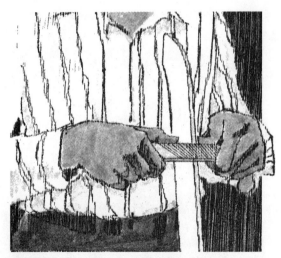

SHARPEN SIDE EDGE with flat No. 10, removing rough spots, nicks. Result should be even edge that forms 90° angle between bottom edging surface and side.

TIP EDGING of ski should not be sharp. Starting even with front end of center groove, round edging forward toward "shovel" tip to prevent tip-tripping.

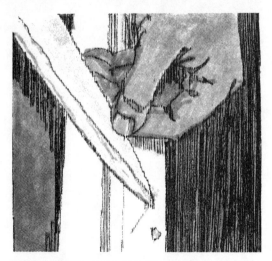

DEEP GOUGES require more than waxing to fill and repair. First use knife or other sharp tool to dig out any loose foreign matter before starting repair.

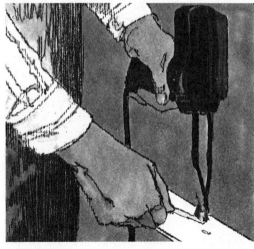

FOR BEST BOND, a clean soldering iron is used to heat base around gouge edges. Molten repair-stick "spaghetti" is dripped in. Extinguish burning drops.

Sharpening and tip edging

Edges and bases take the worst beating. After each trip, knock off edge burrs with emery paper or a file. Run your fingernail crossways over the edges and bottom. If it sticks against an edge, you have the start of a "railing" problem—bottom wear has exposed the inside steel edge corners. To remedy this and other edge faults yourself, get a No. 10 flat crosscut mill bastard file. Then clamp your skis, one at a time, base up in a vise.

Lay the file flat on the base and angled about 45° in the direction the ski is pointing. Keep weight on your thumbs at the middle of the file

and push easily in long strokes down the length of the ski. Don't shift pressure to file ends or press hard. You're working for a flat-edge surface flush with the base. If the base is worn too far, you'll have to build it up with layers of wax.

Next, clamp the ski with one edge up. File the ski edge flat down the ski length to get a 90°-angle edge flat on the base and the side. At the front, from a point parallel to the groove end, bevel the edging as far as it runs up the "shovel" (tip).

Deep gouges and scrapes caused by "fast grass and rock garden" conditions need special atten-

SHAVE OFF excess polyethylene with knife or metal scraper to bring fill down to ski level. Use repair sticks without soldering iron for field patch.

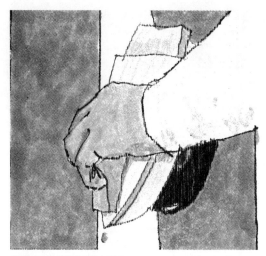

IRON-ON WAX METHOD uses wax held against iron at medium setting. Drips from iron are dribbled on surfaces each side of groove, ironed out smooth.

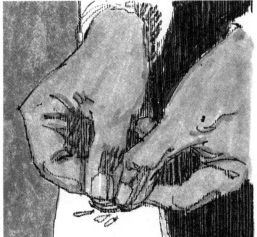

CENTER GROOVE is scraped out and smoothed with coin or knife. Wax runs in during ironing. Keep hot iron moving over bottom during smoothing of wax.

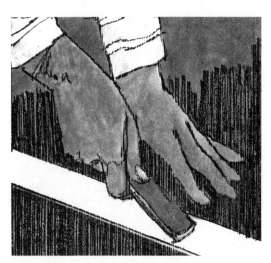

PEEL WAX from edges with plastic or wood scraper to guard against scratches. Full surfaces of the ski are then leveled with metal scraper for even coat.

tion since moisture can work into holes and start delamination. Kofix or P-Tex candles (often called spaghetti) are the answer, and come in colors to match your ski bottoms. Clean base with a rag and benzine or a brass pot cleaner (never use steel wool). Heat damaged area with a clean soldering iron. Split repair candle (for smaller drips), light and drip melted polyethylene into gouge until it's higher than base layer. Smooth cooled material with knife or gadget like a Surform tool. Very gently sand patched area with fine sandpaper, rewax as usual.

Today's fancy top ski surfaces can be scratched, but that won't affect performance. The melamine (finish coat) can chip, but good skis have plastic or metal strips running along the outside edges to prevent excessive damage if skis cross during a run. Scratches can be sanded and waxed.

Your warranty may require professional repair for major damage like delamination or edge separation. But most modern skis can last a number of seasons with minimum—but regular—basic maintenance.

Ice skate sharpening

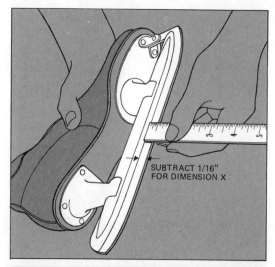

SUBTRACT 1/16"
FOR DIMENSION X

■ MIDWINTER IS THE TIME of year when the kids—and maybe even you—are getting in a lot of ice-skating. And nothing's more frustrating than trying a graceful figure eight with dull blades. By making this simple jig and clamping it to your bench saw, you'll be able to touch up blades with perfect hollow-ground edges as often as needed.

Making a sharpening jig

To make a jig, use two scrap pieces of ¾-in.-thick lumber, long enough to span width of your saw table. After measuring depth of skate blade and subtracting 1/16 in. to get dimension X, cut mating rabbeted edges on pieces A and B with a dado head or make two cuts at 90° with an ordinary saw blade. Temporarily secure A and B together with two small scrap wooden strips tacked across top of jig. With saw blade or dado head lowered, center jig over cutting area across width of table, clamp work securely, and raise spinning saw blade or dado head to make 7/16-in.-deep, ⅝-in.-wide crescent groove on *underside* of jig.

Replace saw blade or dado head with a ½ x 5-in., 80-grit abrasive wheel on the saw arbor. With saw off, check jig with grinding wheel to make certain there is clearance. Determine the exact center of the wheel and mark clearly across top edge of the wheel. Position skate in the rabbet, slide piece B in place, and clamp to form a slot for the skate blade to ride over the abrasive wheel.

Using the jig

With jig clamped in place, raise grinding wheel until it just touches skate blade. Turn saw on and slide skate back and forth over wheel. If needed, wax or silicone spray can be applied to slot to facilitate movement of the skate to and fro. After every few passes, check edge of skate with your thumb as you would when sharpening a knife. Grinding marks should show along full edge of blade. Skates are sharp when, held like a pair of scissors, they cut strips of newspaper easily.

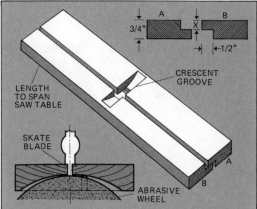

3/4" A X B

1/2"

CRESCENT GROOVE

LENGTH TO SPAN SAW TABLE

SKATE BLADE

ABRASIVE WHEEL

A

B

If the blade has a rough edge to it before you begin sharpening, you may have to raise the wheel a bit and grind off slightly more than usual. Don't forget to give the curved tip of the blade a good sharp edge. To do it, lift the back of the skate as shown in the drawing.

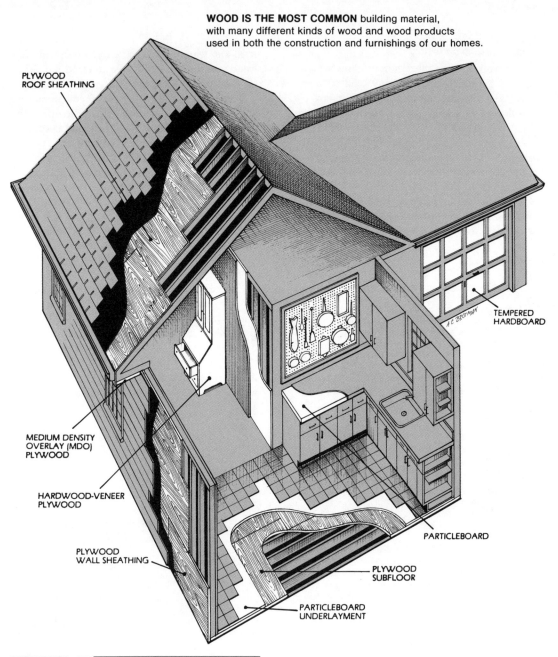

WOOD IS THE MOST COMMON building material, with many different kinds of wood and wood products used in both the construction and furnishings of our homes.

PLYWOOD ROOF SHEATHING

TEMPERED HARDBOARD

MEDIUM DENSITY OVERLAY (MDO) PLYWOOD

HARDWOOD-VENEER PLYWOOD

PARTICLEBOARD

PLYWOOD WALL SHEATHING

PLYWOOD SUBFLOOR

PARTICLEBOARD UNDERLAYMENT

Woods and woodworking

■ WOOD IS ONE OF WESTERN CIVILIZATION'S two original building materials. The other, stone, is used little today. In contrast, wood remains the single most common material for building everything from homes to the furnishings within them.

Woodworking—endless joy

In the hands of an experienced woodworker, wood can take on unique shapes, subtly or dramatically change its color, and be polished to a glasslike luster, for such is the nature of this renewable resource. Wood can be fashioned into an endless number of things.

Wood—endless variety

Some woods work better than others. One species may be stable; another may tend to warp. Some have pleasing figures while others are almost devoid of visible grain patterns. Some are very dense; others are very soft. In between is a broad choice of woods that are ideal for woodworking. These are elegant in figure, strong enough to perform the task demanded, yet soft enough to be readily worked with hand or power tools. When you understand the most common wood species, you can choose the proper wood for each woodworking project.

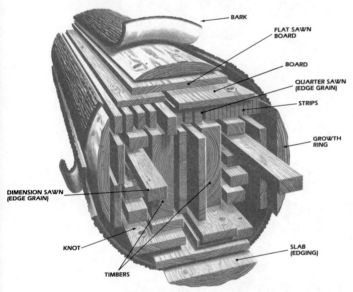

LUMBER IS SAWN FROM LOGS. The manner in which it is cut determines its grain patterns. This shows some of the ways lumber is sawn and some of wood's characteristics. The article in this section about *Picking Lumber* will give you more details.

BUYING WOOD

Your local lumberyard or home improvement center should be the first place to look for wood for a woodworking project. Chances are good that you'll find a small selection of hardwoods: oak, cherry, walnut and perhaps birch. These sources will be competitive in price. Mail-order wood dealers will have much more variety in species, higher grades and various sizes, but you pay a premium price.

Wood grades

All woods are marked with a grade. The better the grade, the more costly the wood. Avoid green wood for a woodworking project. It will shrink,

twist and warp as it dries. A well-equipped home woodworking shop will have an electronic device for measuring the moisture content of wood.

Lumber is graded by appearance and end use after it has been sawn into boards. Boards with a great number of knots will be graded lower than those that are comparatively knot-free. Your application usually determines the grade to buy. If you want a knotty appearance, you'll choose a grade with that desired look.

Hardwoods, on the other hand, are graded as timbers. This assumes that the piece will be cut up into smaller boards than lumber, and minor defects can be cut out as each board is used.

Treated wood

Lumberyards and home centers carry the variety of wood and wood products needed for home improvement projects, including woods that are specially treated to resist decay when used outdoors.

Treated wood has come under the scrutiny of the Environmental Protection Agency (EPA), which has proposed rules restricting the use of

THIS DEVICE WILL ACCURATELY DETERMINE the percent of moisture in a piece of lumber. It's especially useful around the home shop for checking the dryness of a piece of wood before it's used. Wood that's green, or has absorbed too much moisture, can destroy an otherwise great woodworking job as the wood dries. More detail about wood characteristics is in the article *What Is Wood?* that follows.

A KNOTTY APPEARANCE is often desired, especially when paneling a room. You should, however, avoid boards with loose knots like the one shown here. More help about selecting wood is in the article *Lumber Basics.*

PARTICLEBOARD like these can make a woodworking project economical. With hardwood veneer applied, the average person would never suspect that humble particleboard is underneath. General tips on disguising large surfaces like particleboard are in the article about *Veneering* that follows.

certain wood-preserving chemicals. Two types of preservatives are in general use—one is oil-based, the other waterborne. The green color seen in some treated woods is the result of waterborne salts, such as inorganic arsenicals. The wood is submerged and pressure is applied, forcing the chemicals into the pores.

Common sense cautions for safe use of treated woods should be observed:

• Use treated woods for outdoor construction only.

• Wear goggles, dust mask and gloves when working with treated wood.

• Avoid inhaling dust from wood.

• Do not smoke while working with treated wood.

• If possible, work outdoors.

• Wash thoroughly with soap and water after handling treated wood.

• Seal the wood when you use it to construct frequently used areas such as decks.

Veneers

You do not always have to use solid lumber for a woodworking project. Veneer or veneered plywood or particleboard is a good substitute when a project calls for large panels. These are much less expensive than solid stock and are perfectly suited for everything except authentic reproductions of antique furniture. When you use plywood or particleboard as a substitute, you may not need specialized tools, such as bar clamps, which are used to glue up individual boards to form panels.

Veneers are not all the same. Hardwood ve-

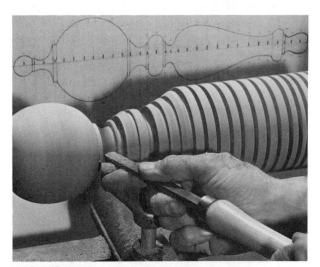

WOODWORKING can be a source of endless pleasure as you shape the wood with both experience and imagination. *The Working Properties of Common Woods* is explained in an article that follows.

WOOD VENEER is available in dozens of different woods. If you can't find them at your lumberyard, you can order veneers from mail-order specialty houses.

neers can be found in rotary cut, half round, plain sliced and quarter sliced.

Rotary cut is peeled in a continuous sheet from a whole log.

Half round is peeled from a half log and sheets collected in sequence.

Plain sliced is cut vertically from the length of a half log and sheets are gathered in sequence.

Quarter sliced is similar, but the cut is from the outside to the center of a quarter-sawn log.

Each type of veneer has different figure characteristics. Sequential sheets of plain-sliced or quarter-sliced veneer are used to make panels with repeating figures. Rotary-cut veneers are most common on 4 x 8-ft. plywood sheets.

DRAW YOUR PLANS

Knowing your project is just as important as knowing your woods. Make drawings of what you plan to build. If practical, make them full size. That's what the pros do. You can lay out each piece for cutting much more easily if your drawings are full size. Tricky curved joinery is easier to interpret in full size. Drawing paper printed with a grid is useful for scaling up a drawing. There are also pantographs to enlarge a drawing to a specific percentage.

Write a cutting list

From your drawings, write a cutting list showing each piece and its dimensions. Give each piece an identifying letter or number and write it on the corresponding component on your drawings. You won't miss any parts if each is identified, and you'll bring home the proper amount of material.

Prepare a shopping list

Use your cutting list to prepare a shopping list. This is important for two reasons: It assures that you buy only what you really need and, if quantity is involved, may be used to negotiate a lower package price from the lumber dealer. List everything you'll need for the project, including hardware, screws, nails and other fasteners.

Help with planning

Admittedly, there are people who either don't have a talent for mechanical drawing or who want to get on with it, lacking the patience to do what has been suggested here. If you're among these, you should know that you can purchase a plan for just about everything under the sun in woodworking. Many of these mail-order plans contain both a cutting list and a shopping list.

Wood for beauty and pride

■ THE LUSTER OF WOOD in a handcrafted project can only be surpassed by your pride and satisfaction in knowing you have done it yourself. These wood selection charts will help you pick the right wood for any project. Throughout this *Popular Mechanics Do-It-Yourself Encyclopedia* there are many wood projects to add this note of beauty to your home; only a few are shown here.

HARDWOODS

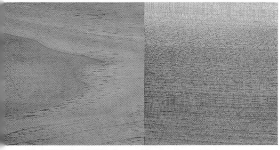

BLACK WALNUT is favored for furniture. It is heavy and hard. It holds finishes and glue well.

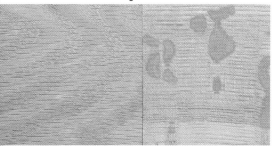

RED OAK has a distinctive grain for flooring and furniture. It holds up well under heavy use.

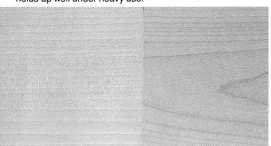

YELLOW BIRCH has an attractive grain that takes a high polish, making it ideal for furniture.

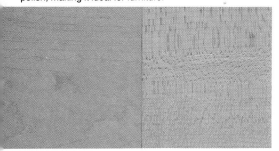

SUGAR MAPLE is good for floors because it resists abrasive wear and takes stain and high polish well.

SOFTWOODS

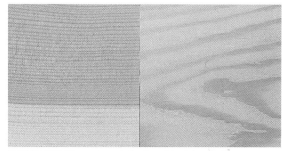

DOUGLAS FIR, strong and shock resistant, is used for plywood, sash and doors, millwork and lumber.

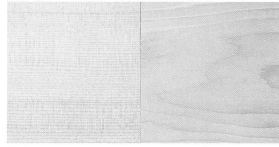

WESTERN HEMLOCK is stiff and light, to be used in construction for joists, studs, sheathing and rafters.

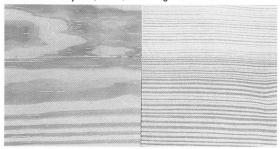

SOUTHERN PINES are used in sheathing, joists and finish work, as well as for poles and railroad ties.

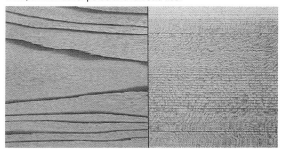

REDWOOD is resistant to decay for use in greenhouses, patios, and outdoor construction.

PINE gives a Colonial touch to this cabinet. Volume 13, page 1634.

WALNUT AND BIRCH INLAYS lends variety to this game table. Volume 11, page 1318.

OAK gives this Victorian sideboard a classic look.
Volume 7, page 856.

OAK has a Mediterranean flair in this gun cabinet. Volume 11, page 1397.

MAHOGANY shines with antique charm in this lap desk. Volume 1, page 66.

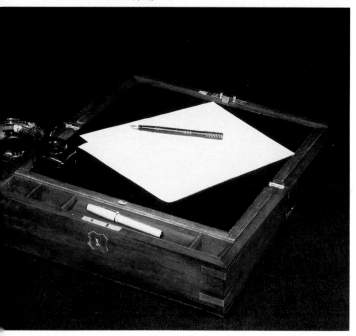

REDWOOD can stand up to weather in outdoor projects. Volume 25, page 3143.

CHERRY adds nostalgic warmth to this rolltop desk. Volume 7, page 830.

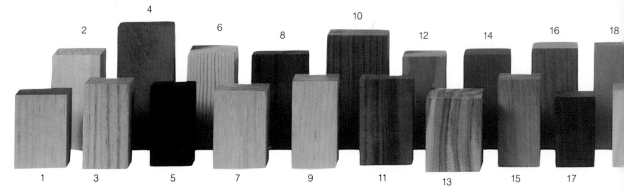

Specific gravity of wood

Softwoods	Domestic Hardwoods		Common Tropical Hardwoods
Specific Gravity	Specific Gravity		Specific Gravity
	Ring-Porous		
	Diffuse-Porous	(Semi-Ring-Porous)	

Softwoods	Diffuse-Porous	Ring-Porous (Semi-Ring-Porous)	Tropical
	1.2	1.2	Lignum vitae
	1.1	1.1	
	1.0 — Specific gravity of water	1.0	Rosewood — — —
			Tulipwood
			Ebony
	0.9	0.9	Purpleheart
			Goncalo alves
	0.8	0.8	Bubinga
	Barberry	Hickory	
	0.7	Black locust / White oak	0.7 Mahogany (Bolivian)
	Beech	Red oak	Teak
	Yellow birch		0.6 Ramin
Southern yellow pine	0.6	Black walnut	
Douglas fir	0.5 Black cherry	Elm	0.5 Mahogany (Central American)
Eastern red cedar			
Eastern hemlock / Eastern spruce	Yellow poplar / Red alder	Catalpa / Stagham sumac / Butternut	0.4 Spanish cedar / Obeche
Redwood	0.4		
Eastern white pine	Basswood		
Western red cedar	Cottonwood		
	0.3	0.3	
	0.2	0.2	
	0.1	0.1 Balsa	

ALL THE BLOCKS OF WOOD on this page weigh the same despite their size differences. The smallest block, lignum vitae (left on scale) is the most dense. The largest block, balsa (right on scale) is the least dense. Density is an important guide to the workability of wood. The table (left) lists the density expressed as specific gravity for a number of species commonly used by woodworkers.

1. Yellow birch
2. Cottonwood
3. Red oak
4. Spanish cedar
5. Ebony
6. Eastern hemlock
7. Elm
8. Teak
9. Sugar maple
10. Western red cedar
11. Concalo alves
12. Douglas fir
13. Stagham sumac
14. Redwood
15. Black locust
16. Catalpa
17. Purpleheart
18. Ramin
19. White oak
20. Mahogany (Bolivian)
21. Southern yellow pine

22. Red alder
23. Bubinga
24. Mahogany (Central Amer
25. Yellow poplar
26. Eastern white p
27. Barberry
28. Black walnut
29. Hickory
30. Tulipwood
31. Black cherry
32. Eastern spruce
33. Butternut
34. Obeche
35. Basswood
36. Eastern red cec
37. Rosewood
38. Beech

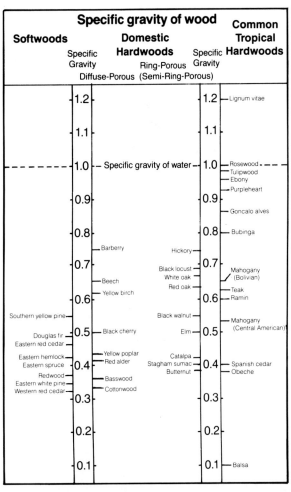

Many offer full-size drawings, so there is no need to scale up.

WOODWORKING TOOLS AND TRICKS

It's not important to have the ideal home workshop containing every woodworking tool needed to make every project. Few woodworking hobbyists ever attain this ideal. Instead, many circumvent their tool shortages through a variety of tricks and devices that help make construction easier.

There are also various techniques developed through years of trial and error that speed work on a project.

Jigs. Jigs of nearly every description help do things that otherwise seem impossible. A jig can change the angle of a table saw fence so the blade cuts to a specific angle. A jig can also hold the proper angle for boring screw pockets into chair or table legs. Another can guide a handsaw for cutting bevels like a professional. A stepped block will help in creating identical dadoes. A simple V-cut in a jig makes boring into the side of a dowel or turned table leg easy, with no possibility of slipping. There's even a shop-made device for creating perfect circles with a table saw.

Boring clean holes. Boring until the tip of a drill penetrates the other side of a board, then flipping the board to finish the bore, makes a clean hole, with no chipped or frayed edges on either side.

Rabbets on a disc. It's possible to use a table saw to cut a rabbet in the edge of a disc, something normally requiring a shaper.

Making cove molding. Cove molding can also be produced using a table saw, when you know the secret for jigging and feeding the material at an angle.

Accurate markings. A V-notch filed in the end of a combination square blade will hold a pencil point while the square is moved to draw a perfectly straight line.

Clean markings. White chalk is better than pencil for marking soft woods if you don't want the chore of sanding the marks away afterward. Chalk wipes away.

While woodworking hobbyists are continually coming up with new devices and unique tricks, manufacturers who produce the tools of woodworking are also busy. It is important to visit the stores where tools are sold and see what's available. You might find just the tool you've been looking for to do that odd task, or find out that a special tool you've been dreaming about is not as costly as you thought.

A VARIETY OF DIFFERENT COVE MOLDINGS that are not commercially available can be made by the woodworker with a table saw.

WORKING WITH WOOD

Certain exotic woods are very expensive and, therefore, prohibitive for use in large quantities. These exotic species, however, can be mixed with more common woods to achieve a spectacular appearance in a finished project.

Layering wood

Just as a cabinetmaker will edge-glue and clamp narrow boards to create a large, flat panel of solid wood, you can join strips of different

LAYERED DOMESTIC AND IMPORTED WOODS gives dramatic contrast to woodworking projects. More about *Layering Wood* projects is in the article that follows in this section.

woods. A lamp base or bowl turned from laminated domestic and exotic imported woods presents a dramatic appearance. Sawn cubes of dark ebony and white oak glued and clamped together produce an elegant chess board.

Veneering

The same appearance can be given to a chess board through the use of economical veneers. Tape veneers can be used to finish off the edges. Veneers can be laminated to either plywood or stable solid woods, such as basswood. Veneers are a particularly good way to use expensive exotic woods. A great variety of wood veneers is available from mail-order houses.

Inlays

Veneers can be laid on to cover a surface or used as inlays in other woods. Pieces of cloth also make fine inlays in some special situations. When coated with a clear plastic finish, they can make the simplest project look like it has expensive enameled inlays.

A SIMPLE BOX COVER takes on new life when contrasting veneers are applied. This is just one of the veneering projects found in the article *Veneering* that follows.

Working properties of wood

Knowledge of the characteristics of exotic woods is helpful before deciding which to use. For example, while ebony finishes to a high polish, it is extremely dense and can quickly dull cutting tools. Teak has beautiful figure, but is oily and therefore does not glue readily. Among exotic woods, mahogany is probably best suited for workshop projects. It has a pleasing grain and is often highly figured. It works easily and polishes to a superb finish.

Bending wood

Sometimes a plan calls for bending wood. Not all woods will bend as easily as will ash, aspen, beech, hickory and oak. There are two ways to make wood bend.

Steaming. Solid wood is steamed or soaked in hot water before bending, then clamped in place until thoroughly dry.

Kerfing. Both solid woods and veneered plywood can be made to bend by cutting a series of evenly spaced kerfs into the back side. The kerfs cover the circumference of the bend, and it is held when the material is nailed in place.

CARVING WOOD takes a measure of skill and a lot of artistic talent. Here's one sculpture that any woodworker can do with the right tools. It's part of the article about *Interlocking Wood Sculpture* you'll find later in this section.

Woodcarving

Carving wood is an art form in itself, and not the joy of every woodworking hobbyist. Still, those who love to carve find endless hours of pleasure both in the work involved and in viewing the completed sculptures. Many popular hardwoods can be used for carving. Cherry is among the best. It is light, strong and has a fine, easily worked straight grain.

Do-it-yourself help

In the pages that follow, all the topics discussed here are expanded in detail, and many are illustrated with step-by-step illustrations of do-it-yourself projects.

What is wood?

WOOD IS COMMON AND FAMILIAR, yet it is a very complex substance. Although wood has been a basic necessity of the human race from the beginning of time, we have come to use wood routinely each day without much awareness of its intricate nature, and its complicated and sometimes troublesome properties.

But for those of us who work with wood, success requires a fundamental familiarity with its physical structure. This helps us understand its basic working properties and characteristics— why some woods are hard and others soft, which woods can be nailed easily and which woods split, or why some woods have striking patterns while others are plain.

Growth pattern of wood

Most of the lumber and veneer we use comes from the stem or trunk of the tree, where over many years the wood has formed concentric layers, or growth rings, of permanent cells. In the temperate zones, where the growing season is interrupted annually by winter dormancy, each annual ring of wood is evident when the inner, first-formed cell mass called the *early-wood* is visibly distinct from the outer, last-formed *latewood*. Woods like basswood that have little or no contrast between earlywood and latewood are said to be *even-grained*. Woods such as Douglas fir having a pronounced earlywood/latewood contrast are *uneven-grained* woods.

As the tree matures and increases in girth, the cells at the central region of the stem cease to conduct sap and become permanently inactive. The outer *sapwood* of this central core is transformed into *heartwood*.

In some species, the transition to heartwood is accompanied by the formation of materials called *extractives* in the cell walls. These extractives are sometimes pigmented, giving heartwood a distinctive color, such as the deep purple of eastern red cedar or the rich brown of black walnut. When extractives are toxic to fungi, the heartwood may have significant decay resistance, as does redwood and chestnut.

It is important to remember that wood is an ag-

THIS BLOCK OF Douglas fir shows how differently growth rings appear on radial (R), tangential (T) and cross-sectional (X) surfaces.

gregate of countless cells, as many as several million per cubic inch. Each cell is a cylindrical unit, up to 100 times longer than its diameter. In the standing tree, more than 90 percent of the cells run vertically. Sometimes, *longitudinal cells* are large enough to be seen with the unaided eye.

The orientation of the longitudinal cells gives wood its very important *grain direction*. Wood is many times stronger parallel to the grain direction than perpendicular to it. Therefore, wood splits along the grain by fracturing the longitudinal cells lengthwise or tearing them apart laterally. Similarly, nail splits or seasoning checks run parallel to the grain.

A small percentage of the cells in wood are elongated horizontally in the tree, arranged in narrow ribbon-like bands called *rays* extending radially from the bark inward toward the pith. All woods have rays, but in most they are too tiny to see without magnification. Because of the structure of the horizontal cellular rays and the growth rings, the properties of wood may be different in the tangential (parallel to rings) and the radial (perpendicular to rings) directions. For example, wood shrinks and swells about twice as much tangentially as radially.

Density of wood

Density (weight per unit volume) is the single

most important indicator of the strength of wood. By knowing its density you can predict such characteristics as hardness, ease of machining and nailing resistance of a particular species. Dense woods generally shrink and swell more and present greater problems in drying. The densest woods also have the greatest fuel value.

The density of wood is expressed as specific gravity—the ratio of the weight of a body to the weight of an equal volume of water—for a number of species commonly used by woodworkers. There is a 12-fold range in density from less dense balsa to very dense lignum vitae. This gives you a good idea of the wide range of properties among the various woods.

Selecting wood for shop work

Functional requirements of a finished project may influence the selection of wood on the basis of its density and related properties. Woods as soft as balsa are limited to uses such as model-making, pinning boards and novelties, where the surface hardness is not a factor. Low-density hardwoods such as basswood, aspen and cottonwood are worked easily with hand tools and can be nailed without splitting, yet they lack the minimal surface hardness for routine furniture uses. Slightly denser woods, such as yellow poplar and chestnut, are sometimes used for furniture, but more often as an interior or secondary wood.

It is easy to understand why mahogany, teak, black walnut and black cherry have been traditional favorites of the cabinetmaker. In addition to their rich color and pleasing figure, the density range of these woods is a happy compromise suited to most woodcrafting—hard enough to serve the needs of most furniture uses, yet not so hard that the wood can't be worked with hand

HARDWOOD GUIDE

SPECIES	TYPE OF GRAIN	RESISTANCE TO SPLITTING	SUITABILITY FOR CARVING
1. Maple	Closed	Good	Good
2. White Oak	Open	Good	Good
3. Birch	Closed	Fair	Good
4. Poplar	Closed	Excellent	Excellent
5. Ash	Open	Good	Good
6. Cherry	Closed	Fair	Excellent
7. Walnut	Semi-open	Good	Excellent
8. Mahogany	Semi-open	Good	Excellent
9. Red Oak	Open	Good	Good
10. Hickory	Open	Fair	Fair
11. Beech	Closed	Fair	Fair

Eastern White Pine

Southern Yellow Pine

SOFT WOOD CELL STRUCTURE

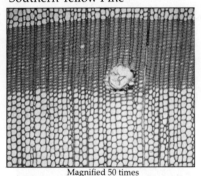

Magnified 50 times

Magnified 50 times

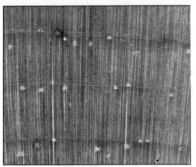

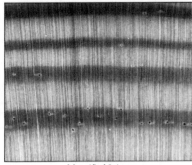

Magnified 8 times

Magnified 8 times

EVEN-GRAINED EASTERN WHITE PINE shows little contrast from earlywood to latewood. Uneven-grained southern yellow pine, however, shows dramatic cellular contrast.

THE PATTERN ON THE SURFACE of a board varies according to the orientation of the growth rings and the degree of earlywood/latewood contrast within the growths. For example, a board which is cut radially across the growth rings, or edge-grained, is characterized by parallel ring lines. The board presents a uniform surface for working. It wears relatively evenly when used as stair treads or as flooring. On the other hand, a board which is cut tangentially to the growth rings, or flatsawn, typically has ellipses, V- or U-shaped markings on its surface. In a flat-sawn board having significant earlywood/late-wood contrast, the surface might wear unevenly. It is more difficult to smooth a flatsawn board without scouring out the softer earlywood than it is to smooth an edge-grained board.

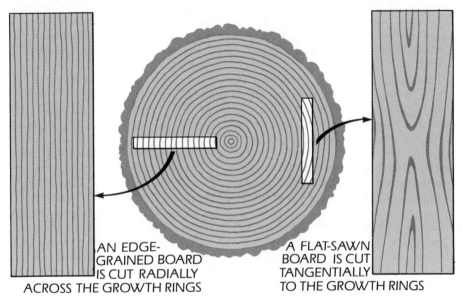

AN EDGE-GRAINED BOARD IS CUT RADIALLY ACROSS THE GROWTH RINGS

A FLAT-SAWN BOARD IS CUT TANGENTIALLY TO THE GROWTH RINGS

HARD WOOD CELL STRUCTURE

Magnified 8 times

RED OAK

BUTTERNUT

BASSWOOD

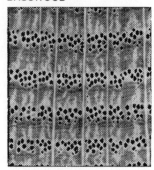

A RING-POROUS WOOD (left) typically is uneven-grained and uneven in its working properties. A diffuse-porous wood (right) typically is even-grained and uniform. The pore distribution on semi-ring-porous wood, such as butternut (center) may produce a striking figure, but usually the wood will not have uneven properties.

tools. Woods in this range cannot be fastened with nails or screws without preboring holes, but tradition has devised joinery methods such as mortise-and-tenons, doweled joints and dovetailed joints.

The highest-density groups of our native hardwoods—including birch, beech, sugar maple, ash, oak and hickory—are well suited to the most demanding uses. They are ideal for production woodworking with machine tools where a strong and durable product must result, as in the posts, legs, stretchers and backs of chairs.

An important message conveyed by the density chart is how misleading the familiar terms *hardwood* and *softwood* really are—the range of hardwood density extends below as well as above the densities of softwoods.

Softwood and hardwood

Trees designated as softwoods are within the *gymnosperm* group of seed plants, in the order *Coniferales*. That is why softwood trees are broadly termed *conifers*. These trees are characterized by needlelike or scale-like foliage which usually is evergreen.

The wood of the higher-density softwood species is strong for its weight, yet soft enough to be nailed and worked easily with hand tools. The large tree size and straight stem form yield the desired long lengths needed for structural lumber in buildings.

Some hardwoods have appropriate density and stem form to yield structural material. As examples, yellow poplar and chestnut were commonly used for building components. We usually associate hardwoods, however, with cabinetry, joinery and other uses where the shorter pieces of clear wood can be used, and where the more attractive colors and higher density provide desired beauty and functional properties to the finished items.

The relative earlywood/latewood contrast—or unevenness of the grain—is the most important factor in producing figure in softwoods. The darker latewood stands out against the lighter earlywood. When a softwood surface is wiped with a dark pigment stain, however, the stain will be taken up more heavily by the earlywood cells. Then the earlywood may become darker than latewood.

In some hardwoods such as oak, ash, elm and chestnut, large pores are concentrated in the earlywood, with distinctly smaller pores in the latewood. Such woods are said to be *ring-porus*. Ring-porous woods are usually uneven-grained. Depending on the function of the item, this can be an asset or a disadvantage.

Most of the volume of wood in typical conifers is the result of a single longitudinal cell type called a *tracheid*. In the earlywood, the tracheids are largest in diameter and very thin-walled. In the latewood, the tracheids are flattened and have thicker walls, resulting in denser wood. Tracheids determine both the unevenness of density and overall density of the wood. Hardwoods have a more complex cell structure than conifers. Through evolution, more highly specialized cell types have developed: On the one extreme there are large, thin-walled *vessel cells* for conduction; on the other extreme there are minute thick-walled *fibers* to provide mechanical strength to the tree. Among hardwoods, the overall density of a species depends on the relative numbers and sizes of the vessels and of the relative cell-wall thickness of the fibers. The uniformity of density is largely determined by the size and distribution of the vessels within each growth ring.

The vessel openings are called *pores* (see cross-sectional views). A wide range of pore sizes is respresented among hardwoods. (Softwoods are said to be nonporous.)

Picking lumber

■ DO YOU JUDGE LUMBER BY LOOKS? Walk up to a bin of 1 x 8s and pick out the two or three that please your eye? If you do, you are in the majority. Most people pick out boards by surface appearance, grain and color. They don't know or care whether it is B&H, sterling or clear. It doesn't matter whether it is western pine, eastern hemlock or cedar. Appearance should be important in any lumber-buying decision. Yet, knowing how wood is graded, how different species perform, what's commonly stocked in what sizes, and the way lumberyards will or won't serve you could save money—and still get you great wood for your project.

Grades of wood

Rough lumber is wood as it comes out of the saw. It has loose fibers and saw-tooth marks. Rough wood costs a little less than lumber that is dressed.

Dressed wood is the rough lumber that's been run through a planer. All four of the long sides are smooth.

Worked lumber is any wood shaped for a specific purpose. Tongue-and-groove floorboards are examples, as are grooved paneling and ogee base moldings.

Kinds of wood

There are only two basic kinds of wood: softwood and hardwood. Easily 90 percent of the wood sold is softwood. Cut from conifers (pine, spruce, hemlock and so on), it's the backbone of construction, most projects, home repairs and improvements.

Hardwoods cut from deciduous (leaf-dropping) trees like oak, maple and walnut go into

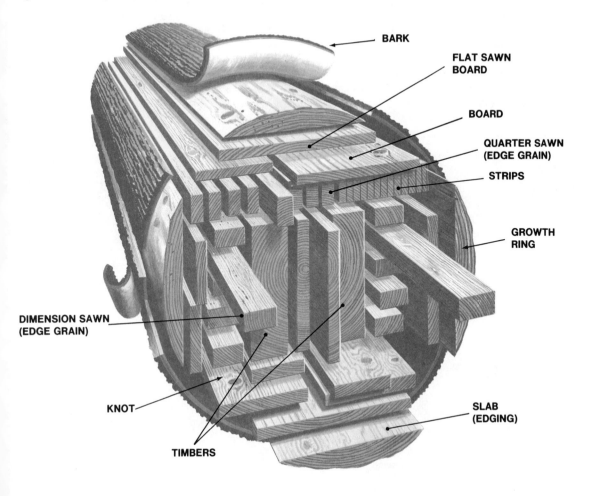

BARK

FLAT SAWN BOARD

BOARD

QUARTER SAWN (EDGE GRAIN)

STRIPS

GROWTH RING

DIMENSION SAWN (EDGE GRAIN)

KNOT

TIMBERS

SLAB (EDGING)

fine furniture, knife handles and cabinetry. As more craftsmen take on these kinds of projects, more yards will stock hardwood. There are also many wood specialty mail-order sources.

Sizes of wood

Actual softwood sizes refer to the dimensions of dressed lumber. A nominal 2 x 4 is very close to 2 in. thick and 4 in. wide when cut from the log. Planed smooth, the numbers come down to 1½ x 3½ in. When you plan a specific project, always work with the actual dimensions of the lumber you'll be using. At that stage, it doesn't matter what the standard sizes are; you care about what you've got.

Measurements for redwood are different, but not by much. Clear, All-Heart and B grades are planed to the same dimensions as other softwoods, but there are two exceptions: A ¾-in.-thick redwood board is surfaced to ¹¹⁄₁₆ in., and an 8-in.-wide board measures 7½ in. instead of 7¼ in. A garden-grade redwood 2 x 4 actually measures 1⁹⁄₁₆ x 3⁹⁄₁₆ in. because it's shaped green and shrinks as it dries.

Hardwood usually is not stocked in easily identifiable sizes at the yards, but check the mail-order houses. If local yards stocked ½-in. boards, two buyers a year might ask for them. A standard 1-in. board can be planed to satisfy any customers requiring differing thicknesses.

Buying lumber

Lumber is offered in even-numbered widths and lengths. If you want a 1 x 7, the yard will rip a 1 x 8, charge you for the 1 x 8, add a cutting charge and give you the sliced-off strip—or you can take home the 1 x 8 and rip it yourself.

Charges for cutting and planing are not consistent. Some yards tack on a small charge for each pass through the saw or planer. Others give you the first few cuts free, and some may cut to length free. Suburban and rural yards rarely cut lumber to project specs. Some city yards, saw to a fraction of an inch.

Lumber language

A *board* describes any lumber less than 2 in. thick and 1 in. or more wide. A board less than 6 in. wide is called a *strip*. *Dimension lumber,* the backbone of house construction, includes pieces from 2 in. thick up to but not including 5 in. thick, and 2 in. wide or more. *Timbers* are heavy structural members. Their smallest dimension in any direction is 5 in.

Reduced to essentials, a good-looking piece of wood *grades* high, a scruffy one, low. Top grades are clear, showing few tiny knots or none at all. High grades have no checks, splits or blemishes. As boards come lower on the grade scale, allowable knots become progressively larger, and other imperfections increase in size, number and importance.

INTERGROWN KNOT, also called tight or red, was a branch that grew into trunk.

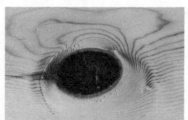

CHECKED KNOT shrank unevenly as wood dried, creating cracks along its grain.

SPIKE KNOT was cut nearly parallel to the grain of the branch, weakening board.

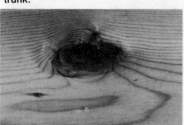

UNSOUND KNOT has surface damage, but it's tight and weakens timbers very little.

ENCASED KNOT is not firmly fixed. It's formed by the stub of an embedded branch.

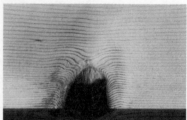

SLOUGHED KNOT was outer section of spike knot that separated near the edge.

MACHINE BURN leaves a black, charred mark that can usually be sanded out.

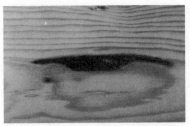

PITCH POCKET is a seam or streak that holds or once held solid or liquid resin.

WANE is bark or missing wood along the edge of a board cut too near log surface.

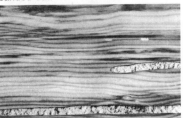

GRUB HOLES bored by insects while tree was alive weaken and mar finished board.

PECK are pockets of dry rot in living trees. They are mostly in cedar and cypress.

COMPRESSED WOOD is on low side of leaning softwood tree. It can be brittle.

When grain is important

Graining counts if you're buying wood for a fancy project. Boards for an edge-glued tabletop must be perfect. First, you want good looks. Second, you need a *straight-grained* board cut at right angles to the growth rings in the log. These *quarter-sawn* boards are more dimensionally sta-ble as humidity changes. A *face-grain* board, displaying long loops of grain on the widest wood surface, is *plain*-sawn, cut near the edge of the log on a tangent with the growth rings. It may show pretty grain patterns, but it's more apt to warp or change size as humidity changes.

WOOD SELECTION CHART

A = High   B = Medium   C = Low

Species	Ease Of Working	Freedom From Warpage	Heartwood Resists Decay	Bending Strength	Stiffness	Strength As A Post	No. Of Knots	No. Of Other Defects
White Ash	C	B	C	A	A	A	C	B
Western Red Cedar	A	A	A	C	C	B	C	C
Eastern Red Cedar	B	A	A	B	C	A	A	C
Cherry	C	A	A	A	A	A	C	*
Cypress	B	B	A	B	B	B	C	B
Douglas Fir	C	B	B	A	A	A	B	B
Eastern Hemlock	B	B	C	B	B	B	B	A
Western Hemlock	B	B	C	B	B	B	B	B
Hickory	C	B	C	A	A	A	B	B
Western Larch	C	B	B	A	A	A	A	A
Hard Maple	C	B	C	A	A	A	B	B
Soft Maple	C	B	C	C	C	C	C	C
Red Oak	C	B	C	A	A	B	C	B
White Oak	C	B	A	A	A	B	C	B
Ponderosa Pine	A	A	C	C	C	C	B	B
Southern Yellow Pine	C	B	C	A	A	A	C	B
Northern White Pine	A	A	C	C	C	C	A	B
Sugar Pine	A	A	C	C	C	C	A	B
Idaho White Pine	A	A	C	B	B	B	A	A
Redwood	B	A	A	B	B	A	C	C
Eastern Spruce	B	A	C	B	B	B	A	B
Sitka Spruce	B	A	C	B	A	B	B	B
Engelmann Spruce	B	A	C	C	C	C	A	B
Walnut	B	A	A	A	A	A	C	C

*Depends on use

Lumber basics for the craftsman

■ LUMBER IN YOUR local yard comes in many classified forms, sectional sizes and lengths. Before you buy you should know these classifications and the various grades and their adaptability to the work you intend to do.

Also, you should know how to make a simple estimate of the amount of material and the various kinds, sizes and grades you will need for a project or for home repair. A few careful measurements—perhaps a simple rough sketch and a few jottings—can mean appreciable savings in time and money.

There are only two basic classifications of *softwood lumber,* but these in turn are broken down into gradings ranging from that commonly referred to as *select* to the *lowest board grading,* suitable only for limited uses.

STANDARD LUMBER SIZES

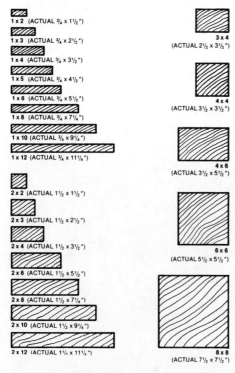

1 x 2 (ACTUAL ¾ x 1½")
1 x 3 (ACTUAL ¾ x 2½")
1 x 4 (ACTUAL ¾ x 3½")
1 x 5 (ACTUAL ¾ x 4½")
1 x 6 (ACTUAL ¾ x 5½")
1 x 8 (ACTUAL ¾ x 7¼")
1 x 10 (ACTUAL ¾ x 9¼")
1 x 12 (ACTUAL ¾ x 11¼")

2 x 2 (ACTUAL 1½ x 1½")
2 x 3 (ACTUAL 1½ x 2½")
2 x 4 (ACTUAL 1½ x 3½")
2 x 6 (ACTUAL 1½ x 5½")
2 x 8 (ACTUAL 1½ x 7¼")
2 x 10 (ACTUAL 1½ x 9¼")
2 x 12 (ACTUAL 1½ x 11¼")

3 x 4 (ACTUAL 2½ x 3½")
4 x 4 (ACTUAL 3½ x 3½")
4 x 6 (ACTUAL 3½ x 5½")
6 x 6 (ACTUAL 5½ x 5½")
8 x 8 (ACTUAL 7½ x 7½")

Select grade

The select grade, *No. 1 clear,* or *A grade* as it is sometimes called, is top quality and is intended for use where appearance, strength and finishing qualities are of first importance.

Common grade

No. 2 grade, or common, has some minor defects with one side clear, and is suitable for general use where such slight defects can be concealed simply by exposing the good side or through the finishing process.

These grades of select stock are again broken down. *B-grade and better* is devoid of any but small, concealable blemishes such as slight off-color veins, usually on one face only. *C-grade* will perhaps have very small, tight knots and possibly sap streaks, and may include heart and sap wood in a single piece. Finally comes *D-grade* with imperfections that can be hidden only by painting.

There is often a further breakdown of common such as *No. 1 grade,* which may contain medium to small, tight knots in great profusion, and other

Nominal and Minimum Dressed Dry Sizes of Finish, Ceiling and Partition, at 19 Percent Maximum Moisture Content.

ITEM	THICKNESSES		FACE WIDTHS	
	NOMINAL	MINIMUM DRESSED	NOMINAL	MINIMUM DRESSED
	Inches	Inches	Inches	Inches
Finish (May have to be special ordered)	⅜	5/16	2	1½
	½	7/16	3	2½
	⅝	9/16	4	3½
	¾	⅝	5	4½
	1	¾	6	5½
	1¼	1	7	6½
	1½	1¼	8	7¼
	1¾	1⅜	9	8¼
	2	1½	10	9¼
	2½	2	11	10¼
	3	2 9/16	12	11¼
	3½	3 1/16	14	13¼
	4	3 9/16	16	15¼
Ceiling	⅜	5/16	3	2⅛
	½	7/16	4	3⅛
	⅝	9/16	5	4⅛
	¾	11/16	6	5⅛
Partition	1	23/32	3	2⅛
			4	3⅛
			5	4⅛
			6	5⅛

WOOD SIDING SELECTION CHART

Material	Nominal Size	Dressed	Face
Shiplap	1x6	5½	5⅛
	1x8	7¼	6⅞
	1x10	9¼	8⅞
	1x12	11¼	10⅞
T&G	1x4	3⅝	3⅛
	1x6	5⅜	5⅛
	1x8	7⅛	6⅞
	1x10	9⅛	8⅞
	1x12	11⅛	10⅞
S4S	1x4	3½	3½
	1x6	5½	5½
	1x8	7¼	7¼
	1x10	9¼	9¼
	1x12	11¼	11¼
Panel Patterns	1x6	7/16	5 7/16
	1x8	7⅛	6¾
	1x10	9⅛	8¾
	1x12	11⅛	10¾
Bevel Siding	1x4	3½	3½
	1x6	5½	5½
	1x8	7¼	7¼
	1x10	9¼	9¼
	1x12	11¼	11¼

quite minor blemishes. It is suitable for a natural knotty finish, such as that so often applied to knotty-pine walls.

No. 2 grading of common may contain more and larger but still sound knots; also more varied blemishes, yet still suitable for a knotty finish or paint. In addition this grade is suitable for rough flooring and paneling where appearance or maximum strength is secondary.

No. 3 grade has some loose knots. Also, there

LUMBER SELECTION CHART

Nominal Size	Seasoned Or Dry	Green Or Unseasoned	Size Before Standard Change
1x4	¾x3½	25/32x3 9/16	25/32x3⅝
1x6	¾x5½	25/32x5⅝	25/23x5½
1x8	¾x7¼	25/32x7½	25/32x7½
1x10	¾x9¼	25/32x9½	25/32x9½
1x12	¾x11¼	25/32x11½	25/32x11½
2x4	1½x3½	1 9/16x3 9/16	1⅝x3⅝
2x6	1½x5½	1 9/16x5⅝	1⅝x5½
2x8	1½x7¼	1 9/16x7½	1⅝x7½
2x10	1½x9¼	1 9/16x9½	1⅝x9½
2x12	1½x11¼	1 9/16x11½	1⅝x11½
4x4	3½x3½	3 9/16x3 9/16	3⅝x3⅝
4x6	3½x5½	3 9/16x5⅝	3⅝x5½
4x8	3½x7¼	3 9/16x7½	3⅝x7½
4x10	3½x9¼	3 9/16x9½	3⅝x9½
4x12	3½x11¼	3 9/16x11½	3⅝x11½
6x6	5½x5½	5 9/16x5 9/16	5¾x5¾

NOTE: Seasoned or Dry lumber has a 19% or less moisture content.
Green or Unseasoned lumber has more than 19% moisture content.

HARDWOOD FLOORING

Type	Size In Inches	Spacing	Nailing
T&G Blind-nailed	25/32x3¼	10-12 in.	7d or 8d screw or cut nail
	25/32x2¼	Same	Same
	25/32x2	Same	Same
	25/32x1½	Same	Same
T&G Blind-nailed over subflooring	½x2	10 in.	5d screw, cut, or casing nail
	½x1½	Same	Same
	⅜x2	8 in.	4d casing nail
	⅜x1½	Same	Same
Square-edge nailed through top face	5/16x2	2 nails in 7 in.	1-in., 15 ga. barbed floor brad, cement-coated
	5/16x1½	Same	Same
	5/16x1⅓	1 nail in 5 in. on alternate sides	Same

Note: If ½-inch-thick subflooring used, nail into joists with additional nailing between the joists.

may be knots of irregular size ranging from large to small and there will likely be more evident flaws. However, the grade is still useful for rough shelving, sheathing, subflooring, and temporary outdoor applications where plain utility is the main requirement.

No. 4 grade is of still lower quality, adaptable to crating and some types of concrete forms. It also is usable in such applications as temporary structures.

No. 5 is the lowest grade and is only applicable where limited strength will serve the purpose and where other requirements, such as appearance, are not a factor.

Special gradings

There are also special gradings for some species of pine, such as that of Idaho origin. The select grades are designated *supreme, choice* and *quality,* and the common gradings *colonial, sterling, standard utility* and *industrial.*

Individual pieces of lumber less than 2 in. thick and 8 in. or more in width are generally referred to as *boards,* while pieces less than 2 in. thick and less than 8 in. wide are usually designated as *strips.* "Strips" as defined where you buy lumber may specifically denote *furring* strips, ie., 1x2s and 1x3s. Actual sizes of furring may be slightly less than ¾ x 1½ and ¾ x 2½ inches. The thickness (¾-inch) may be about 1/32-inch off; the width may be 1/32- to 1/8-inch off. If your measurements are critical, be sure to check the sizes before you buy.

Dimension lumber

Pieces more than 2 in. and less than 5 in. in thickness and widths up to 12 in. are usually designated as *dimension lumber,* which is commonly used in heavy framing. Pieces 4 in. or more in the smallest sectional dimension are called *timbers.* The accompanying chart gives the sectional sizes of those in common use.

Notice especially that sizes given in the chart are the finished sizes you get at the lumber yard. Older sizes have been reduced in the interest of wood conservation. For example, what was formerly supplied as a 2x4 measured 1⅝ x 3⅝ in. These older dimensions have been reduced to 1½ x 3½ in., and similar fractional reductions have been made in the finished sectional sizes of other classifications. The new dimensions must be taken into account when you order, especially if you are replacing old work with new. It should be noted also that dimensions given in the chart may vary slightly due to swelling or shrinkage, and that these "specs" apply generally to lumber cut from conifers, the trees that yield most of the softwood lumber.

Allowance for waste

When you buy lower grades of lumber the cutaway waste often tends to increase more or less proportionally to the price. In some instances you may have to allow as much as 20 to 30% for waste; in other instances this percentage may be extreme even for the lower grades. To save money, consider the need carefully before you buy. If both appearance and strength are factors then you may gain by grading up rather than down. If the need is purely utility then you can often grade down with a savings in cost more than offsetting the loss in waste.

As an example, you need a number of 1x6x8s for edge-to-edge placement, where two-edge nailing, medium strength, and *not* appearance are the main requirements. Here medium-sized and even large tight knots, common surface flaws, and minor twist are permissible.

However, in this order you would have to reject pieces having between-ends slivering, long splits at ends, large loose knots located at edges, any small holes, and excessive twist. The nature of the job may permit cutting out defects and butt-joining ends of shorter lengths. In this case you might buy several extra pieces and still save a little money with a lower grade of lumber, achieving the desired result by judicious cutting.

Hardwood lumber

Hardwood lumber, cut from deciduous (broadleaved) trees, is generally graded according to quality but is also furnished in a variety of thicknesses ranging from 1/8 in. to ¾ in. and in random widths and lengths surfaced two sides (S2S) and four sides (S4S). This is usually classified as cabinet-grade lumber in which small defects are permissible, generally on one face only.

In another classification most of these common cabinet woods (hardwoods) are furnished in a range of thicknesses from ¼ in. to 1¾ in. and in varying widths and lengths up to 48 in., with longer lengths available on order. In this grading the woods are specially selected, rated "triple A" (AAA), in which no defects except the most minor are permissible. All are cut to specified

FACTORY AND SHOP LUMBER CHART

Material	Nominal Thickness	Nominal Width	Dressed Thickness	Dressed Width
Material is S2S; thickness also applies to T&G	1 (4/4) 1¼ (5/4) 1½ (6/4) 1¾ (7/4) 2 (8/4) 2½ (10/4) 3 (12/4) 4 (16/4)	5 in. and wider 4 in. and wider in 4/4 No. 1 Shop And 4/4 No. 2 Shop	25/32 (4/4) 1 5/32 (5/4) 1 13/32 (6/4) 1 19/32 (7/4) 1 13/16 (8/4) 2⅜ (10/4) 2¾ (12/4) 3¾ (16/4)	All In Rough Size See below.

Rough size: 80% of shipment is 1/8-in. thicker than the standard surface size; 20% is 3/32-inch. thicker than surfaced size.
Widths are 1/8-inch wider than standard surfaced widths.
Lengths of factory and shop lumber are 6 ft., and longer in multiples of 1 foot.

lengths and surfaced S3S—that is, surfaced smooth both sides and one edge—or S4S.

Some softwoods are hardwoods

When you buy hardwoods, either from a yard or by mail order, keep in mind that some softwoods are classed as hardwoods because these are cut from broad-leaved (deciduous) trees. An example is basswood, a softwood very similar to white pine in texture and workability. But the basswood tree is broad-leaved and thus the lumber is classed as hardwood.

Some dealers stock both domestic and imported woods, and catalog these by the square foot and in random lengths and widths, surfaced two sides (S2S). You will also find imported woods cut to given widths and lengths ranging from ⅛ in. to ¾ in. in thickness, and in lengths from 18 to 48 in. in length. These are especially selected for color and grain, and are clear with only minor defects permissible on one side.

Special widths

Also there will be special widths in some woods, such as the mahoganies, ranging up to 20 in. Nearly all such woods, both domestic and imported, are also supplied as turning squares and square blocks in various sizes and lengths, both roughsawed and finished on four sides to a given dimension.

Processed lumber

Processed lumber such as cedar-closet lining, hardwood flooring and shiplap, are usually sold in bundles containing a given number of square feet; the individual boards are the same width and, in the case of the first two items, each piece is tongued and grooved. Usually the flooring and closet lining come in random lengths and the boards are matched closely for color and quality. In closet lining, they also are matched for knot pattern. The shiplap comes with both edges rabbeted so that adjoining boards can be fitted flush and level.

Select each piece

No two boards cut from the same tree are ever the same in knot pattern, grain or even in color. The grain, knots if any, surface details and color will only be characteristic of that particular cut at the mill. If your dealer permits you to select for a special project, look for boards similar in color and grain pattern. If you take time to study each piece, you can produce a satisfactory match, but never a precise one. In fact, some variation may even enhance the final appearance of your finished work.

Framing stock adjustments

When you buy framing stock, such as 2x4s, for repair of a wall where you have to fit the new studs into an old opening, it will be necessary to "widen" the new 2x4s to avoid a noticeable dip or depression. One way to do this is to build out the new 2x4 to the width of the old with strips cut from ⅛-in. hardboard, tacked to one edge of the new studs.

Convert a materials list to a buying list

■ MOST PROJECT MATERIALS LISTS are not lumber shopping lists. You've got to translate the materials list into a certain number of 1 x 10s by so many feet long, and so on.

Converting the materials list taken directly from the plans into a lumber-buying list serves two purposes. It produces your shopping list and lets you figure out exactly how you're going to cut and assemble the project.

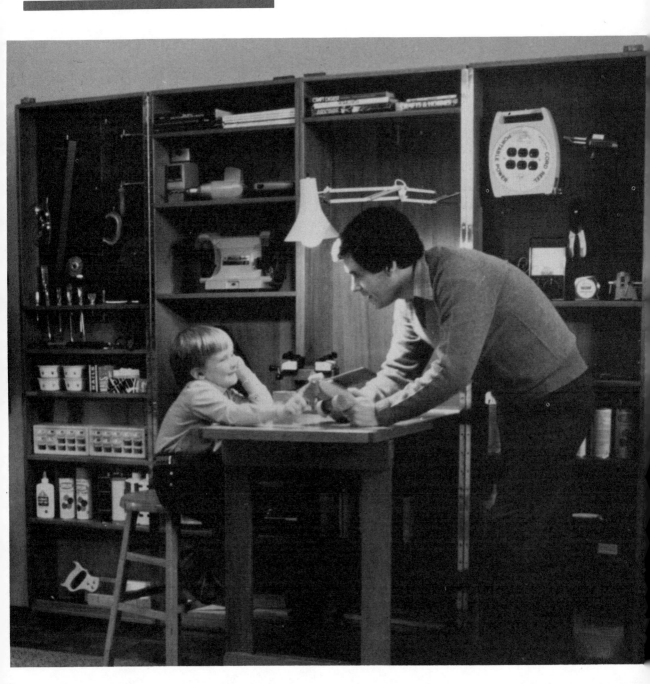

Keeping in mind that wood is sold in even-numbered lengths and widths, start making your list by writing the materials required for each part in one column and the standard stock measurements closest to these numbers in the second column. Leave room for a third column for your actual order. (See chart on next page.)

Using the in-the-wall workshop project as an example, you see the first item calls for four boards ¾ x 11⅛ x 76 in. The closest standard lumberyard size is ¾ x 12 x 96 in. (8 ft. long). This goes in the second column.

The third column becomes your actual order. The first two items are for ¾ x 12-in. boards. You could order four 8-ft. lengths for the first entry and three more for the second. Or, you could cover both with four 12-ft. lengths. Compare prices. At one yard, seven 8-ft. ¾ x 12s cost $81.20 in clear, all-heart redwood KD (kiln dried). Four 12-footers are $72.50.

MATERIALS LIST
IN-THE-WALL-WORKSHOP

Key	No.	Size and description (use)
		CABINETS (2)
A	4	¾ x 11⅛ x 78" redwood (cabinet side)
B	11	¾ x 11⅛ x 22¼" redwood (top, bottom, shelves)
B1	1	¾ x 8 x 22¼" redwood (hinge shelf)
C	1	½ x 3 x 21⅞" hardwood (hinge cleat)
D	2	¾ x 23¼ x 76" redwood, edge-joined (back panel)
E	1	1½ x 3 x 45" redwood (base front)
E1	2	1½ x 3 x 8" redwood (base sides)
F	2	¾ x 1¼ x 21⅞" redwood (rail)
G	2	¼ x 20 x 37" oak plywood (tabletop veneer)
G1	1	¾ x 20 x 37" fir plywood (tabletop core)
G2	2	11/16 x 1¼ x 37⅛" redwood (edging)
G3	1	11/16 x 1¼ x 20" redwood (edging)
H	2	¾ x 3½ x 32⅛" redwood (legs)
H1	4	¾ x 3½ x 21" redwood (braces)
I	1	¾ x 3"-dia. redwood (gravity stay top)
I1	1	⅜"-dia. x 3" hardwood dowel (gravity stay pin)
J	2	1½ (open) x 72¾" continuous hinge (for doors)
J1	1	1½ (open) x 21" continuous hinge (for tabletop)
		DOORS (2)
K	4	¾ x 5 5/16 x 76" redwood (door side)
L	13	¾ x 5 5/16 x 22¼" redwood (top, bottom, shelves)
M	2	¾ x 23¼ x 76" redwood, edge-joined (door front)
N	2	¾ x 1¼ x 21⅞" redwood (rail)
O	2	⅛ x 21⅝ x 28⅛" Peg-Board
P	6	⅜ x 11/16 x 27⅝" furring strip (Peg-Board frame)
P1	4	⅜ x 11/16 x 21⅞" furring strip (Peg-Board frame)
Q	2	¾ x 1 x 2½" redwood (catch plate block)
Q1	2	Heavy-duty magnetic catches
R	2	Brass door handles, Amerock No. BP 302BB

Misc.: Carpenter's glue, 8d common nails (to attach cabinet backs), 1½" No. 8 fh screws (to attach shelves), 1" No. 6 fh brass screws (to attach table hinge to shelf B1), 2" No. 14 fh screws (4, to secure unit), ⅛ x ½"-dia. wood plugs, ⅛ x ½ x 76" plywood splines, 1 standard electrical outlet box, ¼ x 3¼" capscrew with washer and nut (for installing lamp bracket).

Note: Use nominal ¾" clear all-heart KD redwood (actual dimension: 11/18"). Other lumber as noted.

No.	Materials List (in.)	Stock Lumber Nearest in Size	Lumber Order
4	¾ x 11⅛ x 78	¾ x 12" x 8'	(4) ¾ x 12" x 12'
11	¾ x 11⅛ x 22¼	¾ x 12" x 2'	
1	¾ x 8 x 22¼	¾ x 10" x 2'	(1) ¾ x 10" x 2'
1	½ x 3 x 21⅞ (hardwood)	½ x 4" x 2'	(1) ½ x 4" x 2' (hardwood)
2	¾ x 23¼ x 76	¾ x 10" x 8' ¾ x 10" x 8' ¾ x 6" x 8' (edge-glued)	(See order A below) (See order B below)
1	1½ x 3 x 45	1½ x 4" x 4'	(1) 1½ x 4" x 6'
2	1½ x 3 x 8	1½ x 4" x 1'	
2 2 1 2 4	¾ x 1¼ x 21⅞ 11/16 x 1¼ x 37⅞ 11/16 x 1¼ x 20 ¾ x 3¼ x 32⅛ ¾ x 3½ x 21	¾ x 2" x 2' ¾ x 2" x 4' ¾ x 2" x 2' ¾ x 4" x 3' ¾ x 4" x 2'	(1) ¾ x 4" x 12' (C) (1) ¾ x 4" x 10' (Rip in half after ¾ x 4" lengths are taken)
1	¾ x 3 dia.	Cut from scrap	
1	⅜=dia. x 3 dowel (hardwood)	⅜" dia. x 3"	(1) ⅜"-dia. x 3" dowel (hardwood)
4	¾ x 5 5/16 x 76	¾ x 6" x 8'	(See order B below)
13	¾ x 5 5/16 x 22¼	¾ x 6" x 2'	
2	¾ x 23¼ x 76	¾ x 10" x 8' ¾ x 10" x 8' ¾ x 6" x 8' (edge-glued)	(4) ¾ x 10" x 14' (A) (6) ¾ x 6" x 14' (B)
2	¾ x 1¼ x 21⅞	¾ x 2" x 2'	(See order C above)
6	⅜ x 11/16 x 27⅝ (furring strip)	½ x 2" x 5'	(1) ½ x 2" x 12' (to be ripped)
4	⅜ x 11/16 x 21⅞ (furring strip)	½ x 2" x 2'	
2	¾ x 1 x 2½	Cut from scrap	

Working properties of common woods

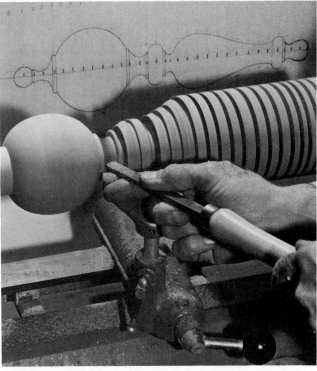

WILL THE WOOD you choose for your project work easily? Check the chart to find out.

■ WHEN SELECTING A WOOD to use in a project, your choice is likely to be governed by two major considerations: the final appearance of the wood after you finish it, and the strength and workability of the wood.

To make a durable piece of furniture, for example, you want wood which is hard and will stand up to everyday usage. It should take turning on a lathe, and take a fine finish sanding. Then, when you apply the final finish, it should offer an attractive grain, take staining evenly, and then take the final finish attractively.

The chart on the next page was developed as a result of experimental work at Forest Products Laboratory, and was designed to provide a guide to lead you to the right wood for each project. You should note that even cuts of wood from the same log vary considerably, so that the values given here are averages.

Under the heading "Planing and Jointing" you will see figures. These tell you the cutting angles which have been found best when using edge tools (chisels, for example, or a jointer or molding head) to shape each type of wood.

The grade of sandpaper shown for each species is the paper which has been found best for the final smooth sanding. Paper of the grade shown will not leave scratches on the surface. On some samples of any of these woods, you may have to go one step finer in sandpaper grade to produce the best final finish.

You can use any color of stain on any wood, of course. The colors recommended here are those which produce a traditional color in the wood. In many cases, the traditional look is actually an imitation of another wood. Birch, for example, is most often stained to look like walnut, maple or mahogany. Walnut, on the other hand, is always finished to look like walnut.

Before making your selection, read the notes in the "Remarks" column, which give you an additional insight into the appearance and working qualities of each wood. You'll find references to such things as uniformity of color, principal uses, and how well the wood can be worked by hand or power tools.

The chart does not indicate the availability of the listed woods. Some, such as pine and fir, can be purchased locally in a variety of size. Most, however, must be ordered from woodworking supply houses.

Fine woods are short in supply and can be hard to find, especially in large pieces. You would have difficulty, for example, in finding top quality walnut in 2 x 8-in. planks. Smaller pieces of the fine woods are available and considerably less expensive. Keep this in mind when planning a purchase. Some of the rare woods can be had only in veneers, and then perhaps only in sheets of 4 x 36 in.

CHARACTERISTICS OF WORKABLE WOODS

General Characteristics   Note: NGR = Non-Grain Raising (Applies to stain)

Name of Wood	Weight Per Cubic Foot	Hardness	Planing and Jointing	Turning	Sanding	Natural Color	Usual Grain Figure	Stain Type	Stain Color	Bleach	Remarks
Ash (U.S.A.)	35	Med.	Good 10-25	Fair	Best 2/0	White to Brown	Plain or Fiddleback	Any	Any	Yes	A tough, grainy wood quite uniform in color. Bends quite easily when steamed. Will take stain, but finishes best in natural color
Basswood	24	Soft	Good 20-30	Poor	Poor 4/0	Cream	Very Mild	NGR	Red or Brown	Not Nec.	Light, softwood usually uniform in color. Fine texture, fairly strong, takes paint well. Used for drawing boards and as veneered core stock
Birch	39	Hard	Good 15-20	Good	Fair 4/0	Cream	Mild	Any	Walnut or Mahogany	Yes	Similar in texture to hard maple. Takes the maple finish very well. Widely used in furniture construction. Fairly Uniform color
Butternut	25	Soft	Good 10-25	Good	Fair 4/0	Heart: Amber Sap: Cream	Like Walnut	Water	Walnut or Oak	Yes	Similar in grain and texture to black walnut. Relatively easy to work with hand and power tools, except as noted
Cherry	36	Med.	Best 10-30	Best	Best 4/0	Red to Brown	Good	Water	Red or Brown	No	One of the finest domestic cabinet woods. Fine texture, dense grain, often wavy or curly. Takes natural, stain, fine enamel finishes
Cedar (Aromatic Red)	23	Soft	Poor 5-15	Fair	Good 3/0	Heart: Red Sap: Cream	Knotty	None		No	Universally used for cedar chests and clothes-closet linings, also novelties. Finishes best in its natural color
Chestnut	27	Soft	Good 15-20	Best	Best 3/0	Gray-Brown	Heavy Grain	Oil or Wiping	Red or Brown	No	Rather coarse grained, often worm-holed. Used as picture frames and sometimes as random paneling. Machines well, takes novelty finishes
Cypress	29	Soft	Good 15-25	Poor	Fair 2/0	Heart: Brown Sap: Cream	Plain or Figured	Water, Oil or Wiping	Red or Brown	No	Tends to splinter when worked by hand or machine. Most durable in outdoor exposures. Will take natural or novelty finishes quite well
Elm (Southern)	34	Med.	Poor 15-20	Poor	Good 2/0	Brown to Cream	Heavy Grain	Water	Red or Brown	No	A good furniture wood but difficult to work either by hand or machine. Takes stain fairly well. Some pieces attractively grained
Fir (Douglas)	26	Soft	Fair 10-25	Poor	Fair 3/0	Cream to Red	Plain or Wild	Wiping or Oil	Brown	No	Widely used in home construction, especially framing. Universally available as plywood in varying thicknesses. Best sealed and painted
Gum (Red)	33	Med.	Fair 10-20	Best	Fair 4/0	Heart: Br. Red Sap: Cream	Plain or Figured	Any	Red or Brown	Yes	Dense-grained wood, smooth texture. Occasional attractive figure in heartwood, easily worked. Widely used in furniture construction
Hickory	42	Hard	Good 10-25	Good	Best 2/0	White to Cream	Usually Straight	Water	Red or Brown	Yes	Among best domestic woods for steam bending, tool handles. Usually straight grained and of a fairly uniform color and texture
Holly	33	Hard	Good 10-25	Good	Best 3/0	Silver White	Mild	Water	Amber	Not Nec.	Similar to basswood in color and texture. Works easily. Can be stained. Once widely used in inlay and marquetry in early construction
Mahogany	35	Med.	Good 5-25	Best	Good 4/0	Brown to Red-Brown	Stripe	Water	Red or Brown	Yes	One of the choicest cabinet woods. Select pieces beautifully grained. Works easily. Takes both red and brown stains. An imported wood
Mahogany (Philippine)	33	Med.	Good 5-25	Good	Poor 3/0	Brown to Red-Brown	Stripe	Water or Wiping	Red or Brown	Yes	Similar to true mahoganies but coarser in grain and softer. Serves well as boat planking, also used as trim and in core-door construction
Maple	41	Hard	Fair 15-20	Good	Good 4/0	Cream	Varied	Water and Wiping	Maple	Yes	One of the best domestic hardwoods. Widely used in fine furniture construction, also as flooring, turnings, bowling pins
Oak (English Brown)	40	Hard	Best 10-20	Good	Good 2/0	Deep Brown	Plain, Flake or Swirl	NGR	Brown	Yes	One of the finest of the oaks. An imported wood, most commonly available as veneer. Very attractively grained. Takes stains well
Oak (Red)	39	Hard	Best 10-25	Good	Best 2/0	Red-Brown	Plain or Flake	NGR	Green Toner	Yes	Perhaps the most common of the domestic oaks. Heavy, strong and tough. Open-grained, used in furniture where durability comes first.
Oak (White)	40	Hard	Best 10-20	Good	Best 2/0	White to Light Brown	Plain or Flake	NGR	Brown	Yes	Perhaps the finest domestic oak of exceptional strength and durability. Beautiful graining when quarter-sawed. Takes fine finishes
Pine (White)	25	Soft	Good 10-25	Good	Fair 2/0	White to Cream	Mild	Water or Oil	Brown Only	No	One of the most popular woods almost universally used for trim, paneling and furniture. Perhaps the best all around domestic softwood
Poplar	29	Soft	Good 5-20	Good	Poor 4/0	White to Cream	Occ. Dark Stripe	NGR	Brown	No	Another of the most useful domestic softwoods. Widely used as a secondary wood in both early and late furniture construction
Redwood	29	Soft	Good 10-25	Fair	Poor 2/0	Red	Mild St. Grain	Red only for toning		No	An exceptionally durable softwood when used in outdoor applications as house siding, outdoor furniture, fencing, industrial applications
Sycamore	35	Med.	Poor 5-15	Good	Poor 3/0	White to Pink	Flake	Water	Amber or Brown	Seldom	Difficult to work with either hand or power tools. Beautiful, flaky grain when quarter-sawed. Most attractive in natural finish
Walnut	36	Med.	Good 15-20	Best	Best 4/0	Heart: Brown Sap: Cream	Varied	Water	Walnut	Yes	Rated by most as the finest domestic cabinet wood. Used by best cabinetmakers from earliest times. Has every desirable feature

Woodworking tips

Big boards from small ones

Not every job requires top-drawer treatment, as in the case of the shop storage shelves shown here. Often, larger stock can be obtained by joining together a number of smaller scrap boards with wood splines to give the overall lengths and widths required.

First, cut the mating board ends straight and square using a planer blade in a table or radial-arm saw. Then, cut matching grooves in the ends to a convenient thickness using a dado head in a table saw. Generally, the spline thickness should equal one-third of the stock thickness. Cut the spline to size, glue and clamp in place.

Neater joints

When you must make a butt joint between the ends or edges of two boards, the mating surfaces should be in uniform contact. Here's a good way to get a perfect fit.

First, make a crosscut on one board using a table saw. Then butt the edge of the second board against the first so both are in a straight line. In this position, nail one or more scrap lumber strips—depending on length of joint—across the joint using two nails on each side. Elevate the saw blade so it will cut through both boards and slightly into the scrap. Make the cut, remove the strips and the joint should fit perfectly.

Miter-gauge check

Don't trust the miter gauge on your table saw to make a true 90° cut. Test it by selecting a piece of scrap wood with two straight, parallel edges. Make a crosscut through the center of the piece and then flip one section over. Press both cut edges together and rest both pieces on the flat surface of the saw table. If the cut is true, both edges will butt perfectly. An angled space between them shows that you need to readjust the miter gauge. A wider space at the top indicates the gauge favors the left. A gap at the bottom shows it is off to the right. Readjust the miter gauge or remark it so you don't have to make trial cuts every time.

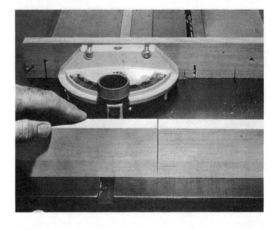

Bandsaw duster

Mount a stiff-bristled toothbrush so it bears against the lower wheel of your bandsaw to keep resinous sawdust from building up and affecting the way the blade tracks. To align the brush, bend the plastic handle by softening it with boiling water. Twist the handle so the bristles bear on the driver wheel. You may have to make a wooden mounting block to align the brush. Screws fasten the brush and its mounting block in place.

Custom drill size

Need to bore an odd size hole? You can easily grind an equal amount off each side of a spade bit that's the next size too large.

Adjust the tool rest to maintain the same angle on the bit's edge. Carefully align tape markers to guide the grinding. Grind slowly and dip the bit in water frequently to avoid drawing temper from the steel. Bore trial holes in scrap to check progress.

Glue brushes

One of the best glue applicators is the small metal-handled bristle brush. Sold in hardware and plumbing supply stores for applying soldering flux when sweating copper tubing, these brushes cost about 15 cents and can be reused many times. For best results, cut the 1-in.-long bristles down to ½ in. long.

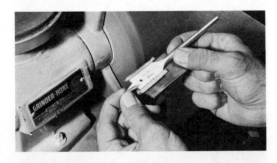

Sanding dust

It takes sharp tools to make precise cuts. Whether you are working with finely honed hand chisels or a high-speed router on just-sanded stock, do a thorough job of removing sanding dust. The dust contains dislodged and fractured abrasive grits that will dull cutting edges. Vacuum carefully, then wipe with a tack cloth.

Marking gauge

A tiny nick filed in the blade end of your combination square makes it much easier to draw a straight line along a board.

File the V-notch in the center of the blade edge just deep enough to keep the pencil point from slipping as you move the square along the work. When marking, slant the pencil toward the square. Changing the angle will cause the line to waver.

Recycle blades

Don't discard broken bandsaw blades just because rewelding is expensive or not readily available. Cut them up to make scroll-saw blades. In very short lengths, you might even be able to make usable sabre-saw blades.

Cut the broken bandsaw blade into sections the same length as the blades for your scroll saw. Using a scroll-saw blade as a pattern, grind or file the ends of the sections to fit the chucks. To cut the blade, hold it firmly with diagonal cutters or clamp it tightly in a vise while making a sharp bend to break it off. Wear gloves and eye protection.

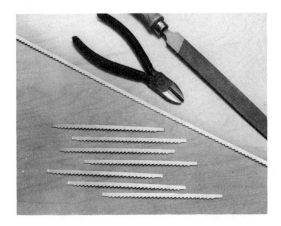

Checking warp

If you are flattening a wood slab using a hand plane, you'll have to start by planing diagonally across the high corners until the top is nearly flat. Check your progress by placing two straight boards of the same width across the end corners. Then sight over the tops of these boards. If the slab is straight, the top edges will line up.

Marking softwoods

When working with very soft woods like clear pine, cedar and redwood, you can crush surface fibers with nothing more than a pencil point. The resulting depression will have to be sanded out before the project is finished. Instead, use white chalk for marking wherever possible. It can be removed with a damp rag.

Square edges with a jointer plane

If you have trouble planing narrow edges square with a large jointer plane, then make the simple planing fence shown here.

Bore two holes in the plane bottom, then screw a straight, square-edged board in place. Cut a notch in the area that falls over the blade to allow for blade projection below the surface of the bottom. Adjust the blade to the proper depth and begin planing the board edges. Use full, smooth strokes and apply slight side pressure to the tool so the fence board always remains in contact with the face of the work.

Clamp repair

If the swivel pads on your C-clamps become loose and fall off, try this method for replacing them.

First, open the clamp wide and place it in a

vise, as shown. Now, strike the end of the screw shaft with a ball-peen hammer to peen the shaft over. Be sure to strike the shaft accurately, for an errant blow could fracture the casting of the clamp.

Once the screw shaft is sufficiently peened, remove the clamp from the vise and position it on a hard surface. Hold the swivel pad in place and tighten the clamp, driving the peened shaft into the swivel pad collar.

HOLD THE SWIVEL PAD in place and tighten the clamp to drive the peened shaft into the collar of the pad.

Glue spreader

Here's an easy and effective way to apply glue to woodworking projects. Take several inexpensive nylon paint brushes—from ½ to 2½ in. wide—and cut the bristles down to 1 in. long. The shorter, more rigid bristles spread glue evenly and quickly. The different-width brushes let you pick the best brush for each job. When you use water-soluble glues, store brushes in a jar of water to keep them pliable. But first apply a coat of rust-resistant paint to the metal ferrules to prevent rust from contaminating the glue.

MAKE GLUE SPREADERS from nylon brushes.

CUT BRISTLES down to 1 in. long.

Screw-eye driver

These homemade tools are great for driving screw eyes and hooks of all sizes. Each driver is a 4¼-in.-long hardwood birch dowel. Make four different-size drivers: ⅜-, ½-, ⅝- and ¾-in.-dia.

Start by cutting a ½-in.-deep saw kerf centered in one end of each driver. Cut the kerf narrow enough to provide a snug fit around the screw eye. Measure 1½ in. down from the other end of each driver and center-bore a ¼-in.-dia. hole to accept a ¼-in.-dia. x 2½-in.-long dowel handle. The handle adds leverage when you turn a screw eye or hook. When driving a screw eye into very hard material, you may need to establish a starting point with an awl, or by first boring a pilot hole with a drill.

TO DRIVE SCREW EYES, cup hooks and screw hooks of all sizes, use these hardwood birch dowel drivers.

Extended pipe clamps

When your pipe clamps are too short to use on a particular project, don't invest in an additional set of longer clamps. Simply extend your existing clamps with lengths of black pipe.

Keep your workshop well supplied with various pipe lengths—threaded on both ends—plus several standard pipe couplings, and you'll be able to clamp almost any project. You're limited only by the length of pipe you have on hand; this procedure works with either ½- or ¾-in.-dia. pipe clamps. You'll obtain more professional results by creating the correct clamp for each job.

To lengthen a clamp, disengage the clamp's tail-stop assembly and slide it off the pipe. Choose the desired length of extension pipe and join it to the "short" clamp with a coupling. Do not use a wrench when adding an extension to a clamp. Hand-tightening is sufficient. Replace the tail-stop assembly and you've got a "new" clamp.

LENGTHEN YOUR PIPE CLAMPS to suit any job. Add the desired length extension to the clamp with a standard pipe coupling.

Masking-tape stop

This simple idea provides a temporary stop for a radial-arm or table saw.

Use a razor knife to make a ¼-in.-deep cut into a roll of masking tape (½ or ¾ in. wide). Position a piece of the ¼-in.-thick tape on the fence or table at the desired distance from the blade. Abut the wood to stop on each cut to produce identical-length pieces without measuring each one. You'll find many shop uses for this stop, such as cutting sandpaper with a paper trimmer. To reuse the stop, peel off the bottom layer of tape to reveal a clean adhesive surface.

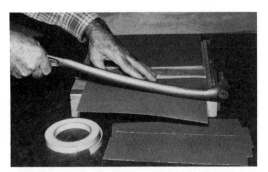

TRY THIS MASKING-TAPE stop on a paper trimmer when you cut sheets of sandpaper.

Sandbagged

Sandbags are a great help when you glue large or uneven projects. They're flexible enough to weigh down irregular shapes that are otherwise impossible to clamp. When gluing large areas of plywood or veneers, pile sandbags in the center to ensure total contact between surfaces until the glue dries.

Fold a 10 x 24-in. piece of lightweight canvas in half to form a 10 x 12-in. bag. Sew sides closed and turn the bag inside out. Add sand until it's three-quarters full, fold the top edges in ½ in. and sew the bag closed.

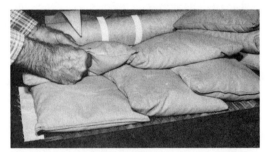

GLUING UNEVEN PROJECTS, such as this tambour door, is easy with several sandbags.

Identifying dowel joints

Correctly identifying and aligning dowel joints can be tricky. Try this method to avoid misaligned joints when you build a frame.

After you cut the frame's stiles and rails, lay them out on a workbench and clamp the frame square. Draw a pencil line across each joint using a try square to indicate the dowel locations. These marks will be used to align the doweling jig when boring the dowel holes. Identify each mating piece with a letter to help you match the joints correctly during final assembly.

MARK FOR DOWELS with a try square. Identify each mating piece with a letter.

Draw knob and pull jig

This homemade jig provides a quick, accurate way to mark knob or pull locations on cabinet drawers and doors.

To install drawer hardware, first mark a centerline lengthwise on the drawer face. Hold the jig with the stop bar against the edge of the drawer face, and align the centerline through the template holes. The 3/16-in.-dia. hole is for laying out knobs. The two 1/8-in.-dia. holes are for laying out pulls. Note that the two pull template holes are 3 in. on center to accommodate standard hardware. You can easily alter the template to lay out hardware of all sizes.

To install hardware on cabinet doors, hold the stop bar on the top of the door, and keep the template edge flush with the door edge. Mark and bore the mounting holes.

To assemble the jig, pass the template through the stop bar's saw kerf and tighten the wingnut. The distance from the template holes to the stop bar should equal the distance from the desired mounting hole to the top of the door, or to the edge of the drawer face.

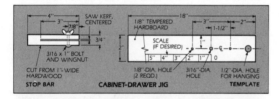

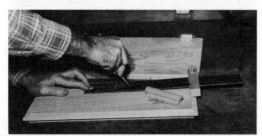

THIS JIG is used to install knobs or pulls on doors and drawers.

Forming cove molding

Making cove molding on your saw is possible by passing the workpiece repeatedly across the blade at an angle. The auxiliary fence is positioned to form the cove down the middle of the work, then clamped to the saw table. Stock is cut away by successive passes over the blade, cutting no more than 1/16 in. each pass. A combination blade works best and produces a smooth cut. Width of the cove establishes fence angle and is

found with an adjustable parallel gauge. Work is finally ripped down the center to produce two strips of cove molding.

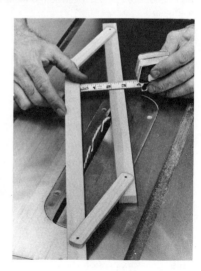

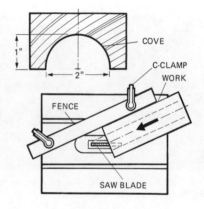

Angle in on screw pockets

Screw pockets for fastening tabletops are neatly formed in the table's aprons with a beveled 2x4 block clamped to the drill-press table. With the depth gauge set for the right depth, the work is clamped against the face of the slanting block. By cutting tangent to the surface, the bit forms a neat shouldered pocket for the screw. Using a much smaller drill, another hole is made in the bottom of the pocket for this screw.

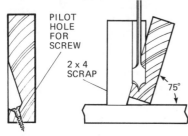

PILOT HOLE FOR SCREW

2 x 4 SCRAP

75°

Rabbet wood discs on table saw

Rabbeting a disc is normally a job for a shaper, but when you don't own one, you can do it with a semicircular jig attached to the rip fence of your table saw. To start, gently lower the disc into the spinning blade, then rotate it slowly with your right hand while pressing inward with the left.

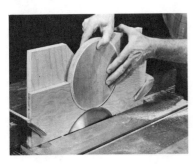

Prevent creeping with sandpaper

Workpiece creeping is difficult to prevent when you make angle cuts greater than 45°. The expert will cement a sandpaper strip to the face of his miter gauge to add a nonslip surface.

Guide your saw for a bevel

It takes a steady hand and a good eye to saw a uniform bevel the length of a board with a handsaw. However, there's nothing to it if you clamp a 2x4 scrap to the top of the work against which the saw blade can bear at an angle as you guide it along the pencil line. The 2x4 must be positioned to suit the angle that you are cutting; the greater the angle the farther the 2x4 must be from the line.

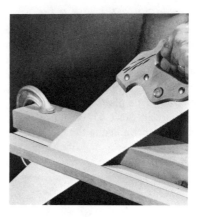

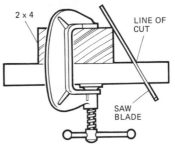

2 x 4

LINE OF CUT

SAW BLADE

Two ways to rip tapers

Taper ripping requires a jig to hold the work at the required angle as it goes through the saw. Details here show two jigs; one a two-leg hinged affair, the other a stepped block. The hinged jig is set by measuring across the legs at a point 12 in. from the end. By opening the legs 1 in. you set the angle for a 1-in.-per-ft. taper. The nonadjustable stepped jig is good for work tapered on four sides, such as table legs. The work rests in the first notch for the first pass, then in the second notch.

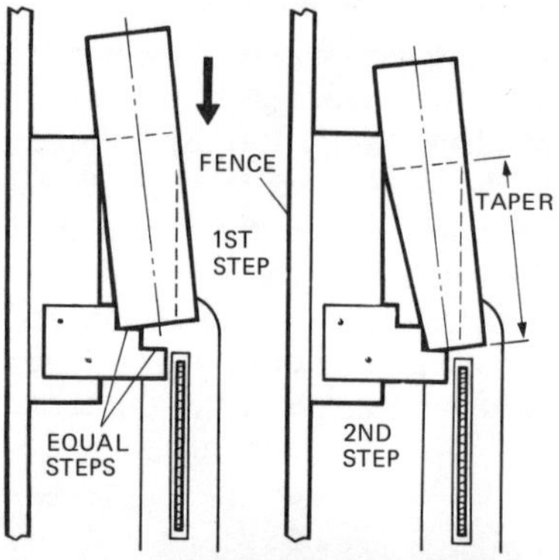

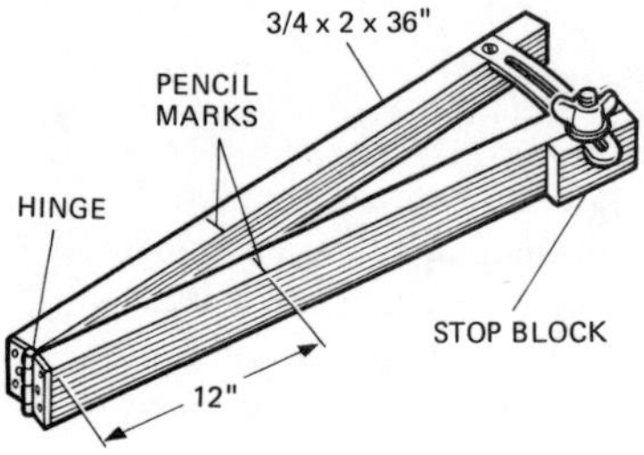

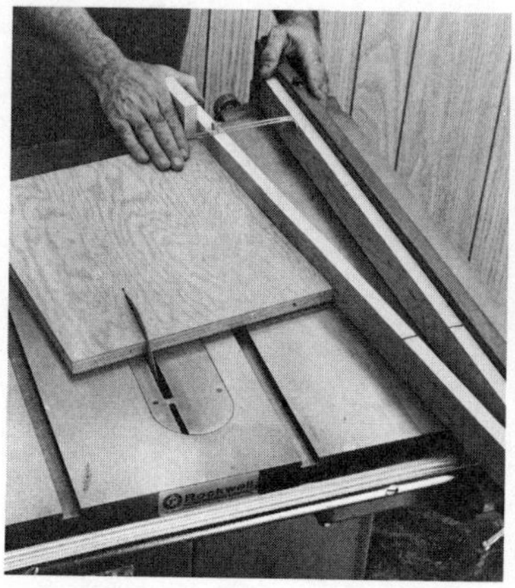

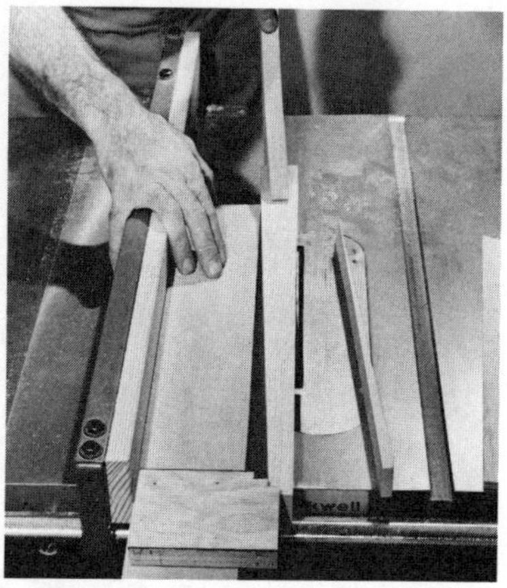

Miter molding faster with a jig

A miter jig is faster and more accurate than your saw's miter gauge for cutting right and left-hand miters. Runners are added to the underside of a plywood platform and the saw is used to make its own kerf. A plywood fence is positioned and screwed to the platform so it forms a perfect 90° angle at an exact 45° angle to the kerf. A strip of sandpaper glued to the face of each fence of the jig will help keep molding from shifting as it's being cut.

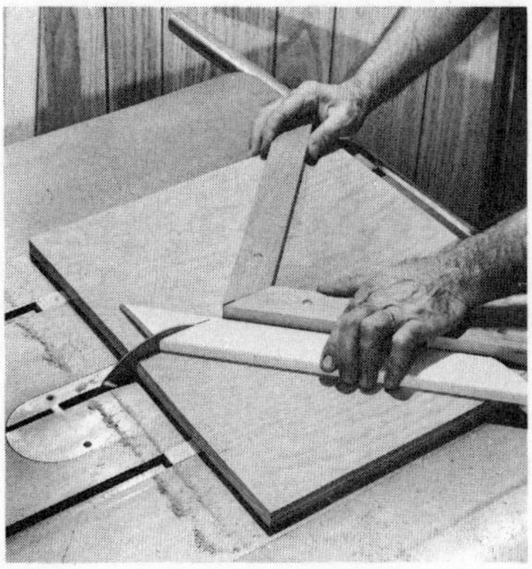

Duplicate identical dadoes

Extra-wide dadoes in duplicate work come out exactly the same length each time if you clamp a stepped block to the left corner of the saw table. Precut to suit the width of the dado blade and the length of the dado, the block determines each successive pass by resting work in the steps. The last step automatically sets the width. You can't miss since the block does the measuring.

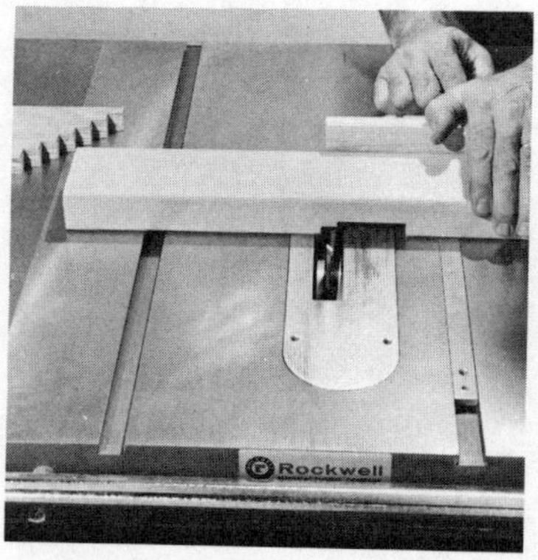

Crosscut wide boards

Place the miter gauge backwards in the table groove when crosscutting a wide board on a small saw. This utilizes all of the table in front of the blade and provides maximum support to the work. After you are halfway through turn off the saw and reverse the gauge in the groove to complete the cut.

Cut duplicates safely with block

Never use the fence itself as a stop when crosscutting duplicate pieces. The work will wedge between the fence and the blade and be thrown with force. Always butt the work against a stop block clamped to the table. This way there is no chance of the pieces getting caught and thrown by the saw.

Board for squaring odd pieces

A squaring board comes in handy for cutting a straight edge along irregularly shaped plywood leftovers from your jigsaw and bandsaw. It's nothing more than a sliding platform fitted with a runner that rides in the table groove. The squaring board is used to support and guide the work as it passes through the blade. The rip fence should never be used to make such cuts. A squaring board is especially good for small pieces. When you want to square-up the edge of a large piece, a strip is clamped to the underside and then it is guided along the edge of the saw table itself. Placement of the strip is dictated by the size of your saw table, plus what is required to true up the ragged edge. If your saw is small in size it may be difficult to guide the work along the table edge without a helper.

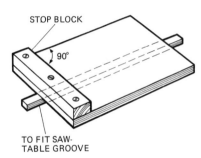

STOP BLOCK

90°

TO FIT SAW-TABLE GROOVE

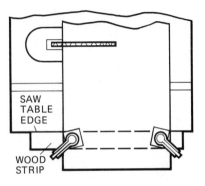

SAW TABLE EDGE

WOOD STRIP

Trim bottom of door with backup

Sawing off a narrow strip from the bottom of a door with a handsaw presents two problems: guiding the saw so it won't run off and keeping it from splintering the opposite side. Both problems are solved by clamping a scrap board to the underside. With the board backing the cut, the saw can't chip or scar the veneer.

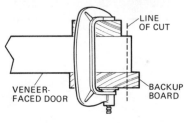

LINE OF CUT

VENEER-FACED DOOR

BACKUP BOARD

Avoid cupping by alternating grain

When tabletops and other wide panels are built up of random-widths boards, the heart grain of the boards should change direction from board to board and the bar clamps should be placed on alternate sides of the work.

Contour legs with a sanding drum

For a perfect fit when doweling legs to a central turning such as the post of a lamp table, use a sanding drum. It works best when both the diameter of the drum and turning are equal. Notch a board to fit around the drum as shown and support it horizontally so its surface is at the very axis of the drum.

Clamp mitered joints

While there are special clothespin-type clamps with swivel barbed jaws for holding mitered joints when gluing, you can make your regular C-clamps do by gluing several triangular clamping ears to each side of the joint. The ears are later chiseled off flush and the surface sanded.

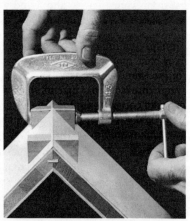

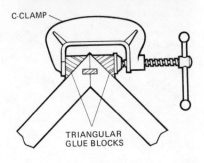

C-CLAMP

TRIANGULAR GLUE BLOCKS

Mass-produce identical work

Pattern sawing is a fast way of duplicating straight-sided work. The setup requires an over-hanging wood fence which is clamped or screwed to the saw's fence, and a master pattern of the part to be duplicated. The points of two brads in the master pattern embed in the wood. The wood fence is aligned flush with the outer face of the blade and the blade is raised just high enough to handle the thickness of the work. Clearance under the overhanging fence must suit the thickness of the work, and the pattern must be thick enough to ride the edge of the fence. The work must be cut up beforehand to the approximate (and slightly larger) size and shape.

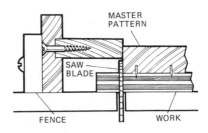

MASTER PATTERN

SAW BLADE

FENCE

WORK

Block keeps handsaw vertical

With practice and a sharp handsaw it's no great feat to follow a line when sawing a wide board. The trick is holding the saw vertically the full length of the cut. When it's important that the cut be 90°, simply hold a square-cut scrap of 2x4 against the saw blade as you continue to saw.

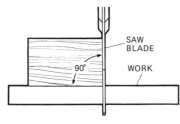

SAW BLADE

90°

WORK

Miter wide boards

How do you rig your bench saw to cut a perfect miter along the edge of a wide board or plywood panel? First you add a wood facing to the rip fence, then with the blade tilted 45° and raised ¾ in., you ease the fence into the rotating blade enough to just bury the tip of the blade in the wood facing. Fence will support miter.

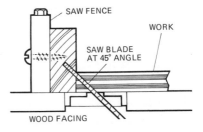

SAW FENCE

WORK

SAW BLADE AT 45° ANGLE

WOOD FACING

Layering wood: a fine art

■ COMBINING TWO or more woods into laminations can produce surprising patterns and color blendings. Laminating also offers a chance to experiment with small amounts of exotic woods that would ordinarily be too expensive.

To prepare the laminate, glue the wood pieces together with a thin, even coat of liquid hide, epoxy resin or other wood glue. Clamp the wood tightly with bar or pipe clamps to form a ''blank.'' Place scrap wood on either side of the blank to protect it from clamp marks.

After the glue has cured, plane the blank smooth and saw, carve or lathe-turn it to form the object. Sand it smooth with coarse, medium and fine sandpaper, then apply your finish.

Be sure all mating surfaces are smooth and totally free of imperfections and dust. Purchase dressed lumber.

1. FANCY TRAY

The handles of this poplar and pine tray are cut from the ends of the tray blank to give a continuous pattern effect. The sides are strips of poplar.

Materials: 4 pieces of poplar and 3 pieces of pine, each 16 x ⅞ x 1 in.; 2 strips of poplar, each 10 x ¼ x ¼ in.; glue; 4 No. 6 brass flathead screws, 1⅛ in. long; sandpaper (3 grades); vegetable oil.

Method: Prepare the laminated blank with alternating 16-in.-long pieces of wood. After the glue has dried and the wood is planed smooth, saw 2 in. off both ends of the blank for the handles. Attach the handles to the tray with screws by predrilling two holes in the underside of each handle approximately 2 in. from each side. The handles should have a 1-in. overhang. Mark screw placement 2 in. from both sides on the underside of the tray, then countersink them. Glue the poplar strips to the tray sides. Sand smooth, then finish with oil.

2. ROLLING PIN

This rolling pin is made of maple and teak discs turned on a lathe.

Materials: 10 maple and 9 teak discs each 4 in. in diameter by ¹³⁄₁₆ in. thick; 2½-in.-square teak stock about 8 in. long; glue; ¼-in.-diameter dowel; 2 sockethead screws ⅝-18 x 13 in. and

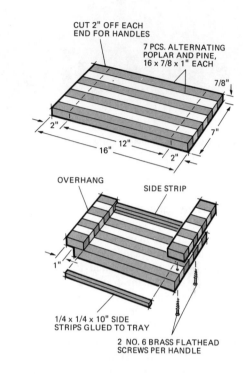

CUT 2" OFF EACH END FOR HANDLES

7 PCS. ALTERNATING POPLAR AND PINE, 16 x 7/8 x 1" EACH

7/8"

2"

12"

16"

7"

2"

OVERHANG

SIDE STRIP

1"

1/4 x 1/4 x 10" SIDE STRIPS GLUED TO TRAY

2 NO. 6 BRASS FLATHEAD SCREWS PER HANDLE

USE A dowel as an axle while you are sanding discs.

A

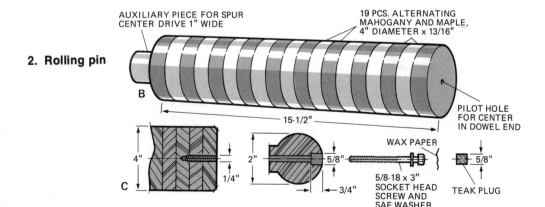

2. Rolling pin

AUXILIARY PIECE FOR SPUR CENTER DRIVE 1" WIDE

19 PCS. ALTERNATING MAHOGANY AND MAPLE, 4" DIAMETER x 13/16"

B

15-1/2"

PILOT HOLE FOR CENTER IN DOWEL END

4"

1/4"

C

2"

5/8"

3/4"

WAX PAPER

5/8-18 x 3" SOCKET HEAD SCREW AND SAE WASHER

TEAK PLUG

5/8"

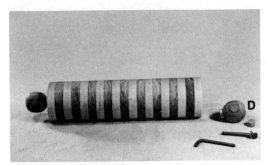

THE ROLLING pin is finally ready to be assembled.

SAE washers; sandpaper; wax paper; peanut oil.

Method: On a jigsaw cut out the 19 discs. Drill a ¼-in. center hole in each (A). Using a dowel as an axle, individually sand the disc edges. Cut the dowel to equal the combined thickness of the discs plus 1-in. Slide the discs onto the dowel and glue together with an auxiliary piece of wood to serve as the spur center drive (B). (You may want to enlarge the disc holes to ⁹⁄₃₂ in.) When dry, lay out the center on the drive piece, mount and turn. Remove the auxiliary spur drive and clean the glue from the rolling pin end. Turn the teak stock to a 2-in. diameter and saw crosswise in half for the handles. Drill pilot holes through both handles and make a ⅝-in.-diameter counterbore in one end of each handle ¾ in. deep. Drill pilot hole to ¹¹⁄₃₂ in. on each handle. Cut two teak plugs ⅝ in. diameter by ¾ in. deep. Drill ¼ in. by 2 in. deep into each roller end and make a ⁵⁄₁₆-18 coarse thread tap (C). With a cotton swab place five-minute epoxy glue into the threads in the roller ends, being careful not to get any on the outside face. Add wax paper over the screwheads or the roller may not rotate. Assemble using PVA (polyvinyl acetate) glue for the plug (D). Finish with oil.

USE A WOOD RASP to shape the laminated salad scoops.

3. SALAD SCOOPS

These salad scoops are made with five layers of reddish Padouk veneer.

Materials: 5 pieces 9 x 11-in. veneer ¹⁄₂₈-in. thick; casein glue; lead pipe about 3-in. diameter and 11 in. long (or other cylindrical form); rubber strips for clamping (from an inner tube or rubber gloves); 2 6-in. pieces of leather lacing; vegetable oil.

Method: Cut the veneer pieces, then sponge with water until pliable. Glue them together with an even coat of glue. Clamp the veneer around a pipe, securing it with the rubber bands until the veneer is dry. It will form a nearly complete cylinder (A). Remove from pipe and saw into two equal pieces (B). Trace the full-size pattern (C) on a veneer piece and saw to rough shape with a coping saw. Trace pattern on reverse side of paper as guide for second scoop to produce a right and left-hand scoop. Refine with wood rasp. Sand, then oil. Drill holes for leather hangers.

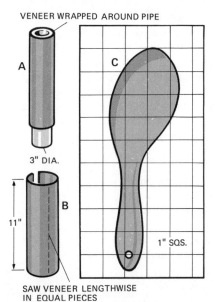

VENEER WRAPPED AROUND PIPE

A 3" DIA.

11"

B

SAW VENEER LENGTHWISE IN EQUAL PIECES

C

1" SQS.

4. BREADBOARD

This poplar and pine breadboard has a handle carved from walnut.

Materials: 4 pieces of poplar and 3 pieces pine, each 11 x 1 x ⅞ in.; 1 piece of walnut 10 x 2½ x 2¾ in.; glue; sandpaper; 2 No. 6 brass flathead screws 1⅛ in. long; mineral oil.

Method: Prepare laminated blank with alternating wood pieces. After the glue has dried, plane smooth. Rough-shape the handle end of the board with a saw (A), and sand smooth. Rough-shape the handle with a saw (B). Round with a ½-in. wood gouge and a wood rasp. Sand smooth. Join handle and board by carefully predrilling screw holes in the underside of the handle, marking off screw placement on the underside of the board and countersinking them. Finish with oil.

5. STRIPED BOWL

Angled mahogany and maple pieces form a striking pattern.

Materials: 10 mahogany and 9 maple pieces, each ¹³⁄₁₆ x 7½ x 13 in.; sandpaper; glue; peanut oil.

Method: To prepare the laminted blank, mark and saw off at 30° angles the ends of the wood on the 7½-in. dimension (A). Glue alternate types of wood together and clamp. The laminated blank will not have vertical sides (B). Saw off the slanted sides to form a rectangle (C). Locate the center of the blank. Mark off both center auxiliary faceplate circle and top outside bowl diameter (14¼ in.) plus ½ in. on the blank. Use a bandsaw to form a thick disc the diameter of the bowl top plus ½ in. (D). Attach auxiliary plate to faceplate and screw to bowl. Mount on lathe and turn the outside of the bowl. Reverse and turn inside of bowl (E). Sand, then oil.

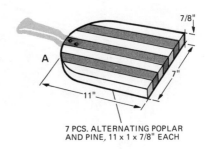

7 PCS. ALTERNATING POPLAR AND PINE, 11 x 1 x 7/8" EACH

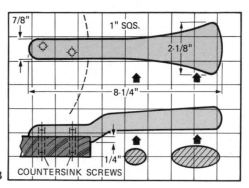

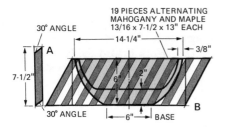

RECTANGULAR blank is bandsawed to form thick disc equal to outside diameter of bowl top (14¼ in.) plus ½ in.

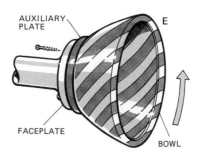

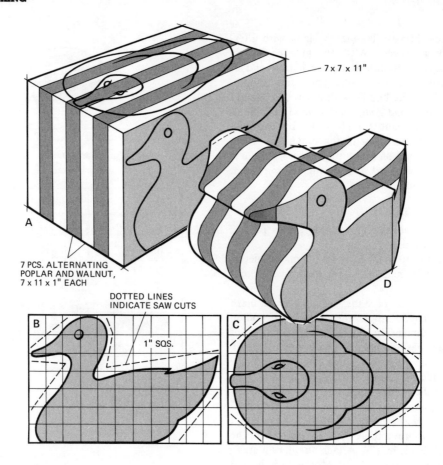

7 x 7 x 11"

7 PCS. ALTERNATING
POPLAR AND WALNUT,
7 x 11 x 1" EACH

DOTTED LINES
INDICATE SAW CUTS

1" SQS.

6. DUCK

This poplar and walnut duck is a reward for a craftsman.

Materials: 4 poplar and 3 walnut pieces each 7 x 11 x 1 in., glue; 15-in. square plywood; 2 screws; ¾ and ½-in. wood gouges; rasp; sandpaper; linseed oil; butcher's wax.

Method: Prepare the blank and plane smooth. Draw the duck on the blank (A). Form the side of the duck by cutting with a saw (B). Secure the duck to the work surface. Fasten it to the plywood square with screws and clamp the plywood to the work surface. Refine sides with gouges. Redraw and form top (C) with saw and gouges. The rough shape should look similar to the drawing (D). Work toward the back and shape tail. Level bumps and gouge marks with rasp. Sand smooth. Apply three coats of oil. Remove excess oil and apply wax.

Bending wood

■ PERHAPS YOU HAVE ADMIRED a fine example of bent woodwork and said to yourself, "If I could only do that . . ." You can. Just look at the two photos below that picture examples of wood bending done with simple, inexpensive equipment that can be assembled by any craftsman. You probably already have some of the necessary equipment such as the household iron, shown in use in bending plywood in Fig. 1, or the radial saw and bandsaw used in kerfing, Figs. 7, 8, and 9. But for kerf bending you don't even need these power tools. Kerfing can be done with a backsaw, using a guide to make sure all the cuts are square across the stock and are made to a uniform depth.

APPLYING HEAT with an electric iron will cause ¼-in. plywood to take a moderate bend. Fasten as you go. Ringed nails work best for this job; they are tough to pull out.

2 **SOLID WOOD** can be bent by kerfing, steaming, boiling or with cauls. Bending by kerfing is well known to old-time carpenters, also cabinet-makers and millwork fabricators.

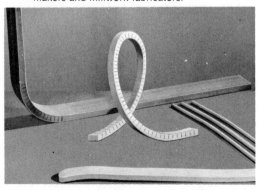

3 **AN EXAMPLE** of wood bending by lamination of layers of thin stock joined layer by layer with glue. Piece will hold bend even though left freestanding, as shown by arms of this chair.

4 **LONG STRIPS** and even wide boards can be bent by soaking or heating part to be bent and staking on any level area in the yard until dry. Degree of bend should be over that required to allow for spring-back. Use wooden stakes.

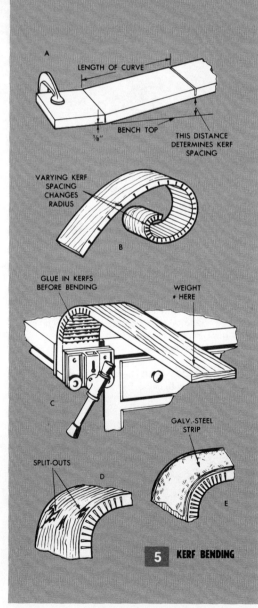

Some kinds of wood bend more readily than others. For example, hickory which has been properly prepared by heating, soaking or steaming, will bend almost back on itself without splintering or breaking. Ash, properly prepared, will bend quite easily. This also is quite generally true of the domestic oaks. On the other hand, the more dense, fine-grained woods such as birch and maple are more difficult to bend in the solid. If you build up to a required thickness by gluing and laminating thin strips of these woods, then bending them is easily done by clamping the strips between shaped cauls, as in the various methods of caul bending, Fig. 18. You can put a sweeping bend in a long strip or board simply by soaking the piece and staking out in the yard as in Fig. 4.

Old-time carpenters and interior trimmers were familiar with the method of kerf bending, Fig. 5. The trick in obtaining the degree of curvature desired is in the spacing, number and depth of the kerfs. As you can see in Fig. 5, detail B, the curvature can be varied by spacing of the kerfs. And the bend can be easily held by applying glue in the kerfs before bending as in detail C, Fig. 5. To determine the space between kerfs you work from the known radius. The bend you plan to make is an arc of a circle. First, determine the circumference of the circle. Then divide 360 by the number of degrees that will be included in the bend (arc). As an example, for a right-angle bend divide 360 by 90. The answer, of course, is 4. Divide the length of the circumference by 4 and the

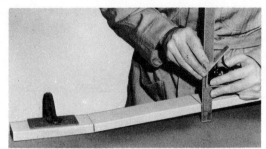

6 **METHOD** of measuring spacing of kerfs. Raise stock until kerf at left closes. Then measure as shown, using a combination square.

7 **KERFING** is easily done with a bandsaw. Note guide is set at slight angle so stock will clear

8 **KERFING** also is easily and quickly done with a radial saw. Here spaced kerfs are cut square across as stock is pushed along fence.

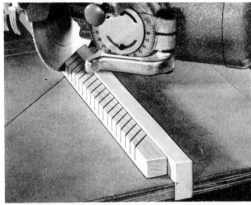

9 **KERFING** stock at an angle results in an advancing spiral bend as in center of photo, Fig. 2. This is done with a radial saw.

answer will be the length of the curve you desire. Mark this distance, or length, on the work where the curve is to be and make the first kerf at one end of the portion that is to be curved. Then clamp the board to a table or bench as in A, Fig. 5, and Fig. 6. Raise the end opposite the kerf until the edges of the kerf meet. Then measure the distance from the lower edge of the board (a second kerf is shown in detail A at this point) to the bench top and you've got the spacing of the kerfs for that particular job.

Kerfing at an angle with the center line of the work, Fig. 9, will give you an advancing spiral form of the type shown at the center of the photo, Fig. 2. In making a right-angle bend, or when making a fairly sharp bend past a right angle, you may have trouble with split-outs on the convex face, Fig. 5, detail D. This usually can be overcome by strapping with a strip of galvanized steel as in Fig. 5 detail E, also detail B, Fig. 18. The metal strap must extend the full length of the work and be clamped at the ends before the bend is made. As the work shortens in

bending, the strap will be drawn very tight. This will prevent any split-outs by forcing the surface fibers to take the bend. After the work has thoroughly dried and the fibers have taken a set, split-outs are unlikely. Surface as in Fig. 10.

Plywood, ¼ in. and less in thickness, can be made to take a bend quite easily by alternately sponging and ironing a small area as in Fig. 1. The material is nailed or screwed in place as you go. Apply pressure and keep the iron moving so that its heat is distributed as uniformly as possible over the sponged area.

Short strips of any of the bendable woods, also sections of long strips such as boat chines, can be bent by steaming as in Fig. 11 and in Fig. 12, details A and B. Anything you can devise from materials at hand which will partially confine the steam will serve the purpose. Fig. 11 and detail A, Fig. 12 suggest methods of steaming small pieces. Although necessarily rather crude, both methods are, nevertheless, effective. Note that in both units steam is generated in a separate container, or "boiler," and piped to the steam box.

A length of box gutter or a length of square downspout is excellent for steaming long pieces.

Another simpler method of steaming small strips is shown in detail B, Fig. 12. Anything that will hold water, or that can be made to hold water, will do—a length of pipe capped at one end as shown, tubing closed at one end, or even a 3 or 4-in. vent pipe sealed at the joints and capped. Still another method is detailed at C in Fig. 12. Here the stock is subjected to boiling water for 20 min. to a half hour. Use a 55-gal. drum for long pieces, an ordinary wash boiler for short strips.

Caul bending, Figs. 15 through 18, provides a means of bending either thin solid stock, the toboggan slats in Fig. 17 being one example, and the bending of panels or strips laminated from several thicknesses of thin material, Figs. 15, 16 and 18. Detail A, Fig. 18 is a common, workable method of bending a laminate, which consists of several thicknesses of thin stock (veneers in regular thicknesses can be used) glued together and clamped to the form as indicated. Detail B, Fig. 18 shows the method of making toboggan slats and similar bent parts, also pictured in Fig. 17. A reverse-curve bend can be cauled as in Fig. 18.

10 **AFTER BENDING,** tension, or face, side of stock is finished by sanding. Be careful not to cut through to the saw kerfs.

11 **SIMPLE SETUP** for steaming short strips of solid stock. Steam source is 1-gal. can serving as "boiler." Don't let it run dry.

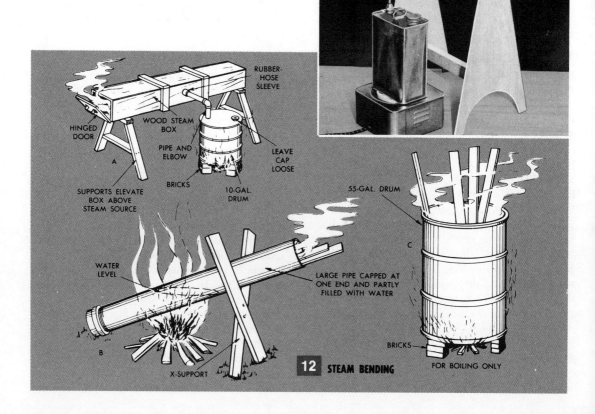

12 **STEAM BENDING**

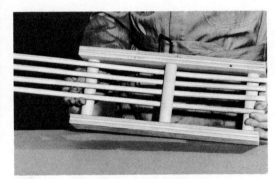

13 **OLD METHOD** of bending chair slats (or splats) and rounds. Stock to be bent is steamed or soaked. See sketch below for bending.

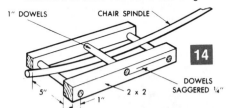

1" DOWELS CHAIR SPINDLE

14

DOWELS SAGGERED ¼"

5" 1" 2 x 2

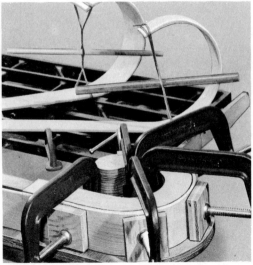

17 **FORM BENDING** is a method commonly used to produce toboggan slats requiring extreme bends. Pad clamps to protect slats.

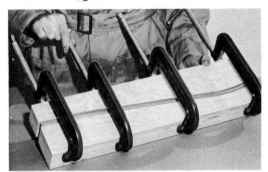

15 **BENDING LAMINATED STOCK** is best done with cauls built up from several thicknesses of plywood. Pressure on C-clamps should be even.

16 **CAUL BENDING** of a panel, the laminations being joined with glue. When dry, panel will hold bend. Frame is made of hardwood.

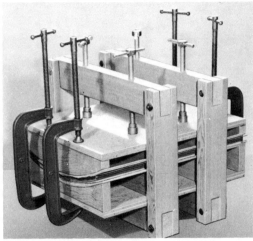

Material can be made to take an edgewise bend by first bandsawing a kerf on the center line as in Fig. 18, detail D, and then steaming and bending around a form. After the piece has dried on the form, the kerf can be opened and glue applied and the work clamped until dry. Details E and G show built-up cauls for laminating small panels, both convex and concave forms. When laminating stock in this manner, apply glue to the laminations and then drive a brad near each end as in detail F. This will prevent the laminations from shifting when the cauls are clamped together, Fig. 3 and 16.

An old method of setting a bend in chair rounds (an example is the bend in the back rounds of the Boston rocker) is pictured in Fig. 13 and detailed in Fig. 14. Thin, flat stock also can be bent in this form, Fig. 14. When flat stock is bent in such a form, or bending jig, 1 x 2s with one face slightly rounded are usually substituted for the round dowels. Pieces so shaped give a more uniform bend in flat stock.

Domestic woods which can be made to take a bend quite easily by the methods outlined include ash, hickory, elm, birch, maple, red gum, oak and beech. Of these only ash, hickory and elm will take the more extreme bends. Only straight-grained stock in any of these woods is suitable for bending. Only the fir plywoods can be bent moderately by use of heat.

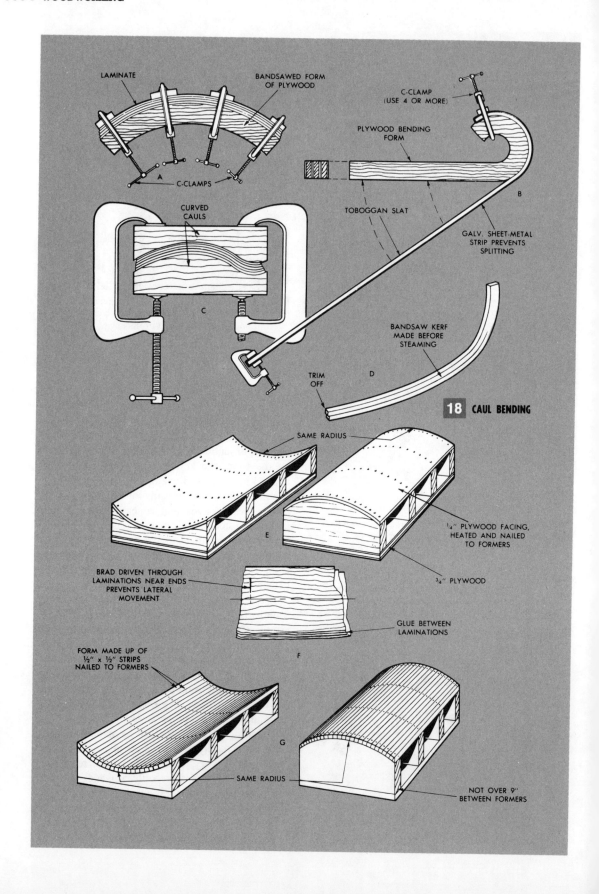

LAMINATE

BANDSAWED FORM OF PLYWOOD

C-CLAMP (USE 4 OR MORE)

PLYWOOD BENDING FORM

A

C-CLAMPS

TOBOGGAN SLAT

B

GALV. SHEET-METAL STRIP PREVENTS SPLITTING

CURVED CAULS

C

BANDSAW KERF MADE BEFORE STEAMING

TRIM OFF

D

18 CAUL BENDING

SAME RADIUS

E

¼" PLYWOOD FACING, HEATED AND NAILED TO FORMERS

¾" PLYWOOD

BRAD DRIVEN THROUGH LAMINATIONS NEAR ENDS PREVENTS LATERAL MOVEMENT

GLUE BETWEEN LAMINATIONS

F

FORM MADE UP OF ½" x ½" STRIPS NAILED TO FORMERS

G

SAME RADIUS

NOT OVER 9" BETWEEN FORMERS

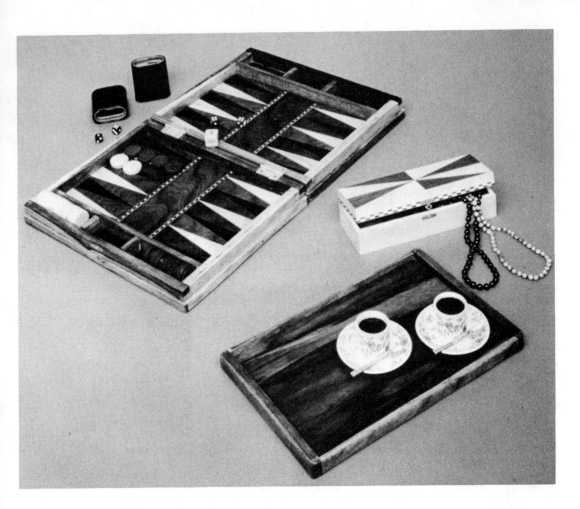

Veneering: beautiful wood on a budget

■ YOU CAN BUILD the intriguing markings and the meandering grain patterns of exotic hardwoods into your projects once you know the secrets of veneering. These wafers of wood offer an inexpensive way to give unfinished furniture and humble surfaces the rich look of hardwood. Veneers can also counteract warpage when they're applied to both sides of a panel. Since you can select the veneer pieces that join together, you can create patterns in wood; for example, a book match design where two sides are mirror images from the center. You can also join four pieces of veneer so their grain forms a diamond shape. Veneers usually come in ½8 to ⅓6-in. thicknesses in sheets from 4 to 12-in. wide and 3 ft. or longer.

INLAY BOX

With a little effort and *not* much money you can turn an inexpensive basswood box from a craft shop into a unique and elegant box for jewelry or odds and ends by applying veneer. You can make the top design by cutting two light and two dark rectangles, halving them diagonally and joining the pieces together, alternating wood types.

Materials include a box, light and dark veneer, fancy inlay border, hinges, lock, veneer tape, contact adhesive, No. 180 garnet paper and varnish or other finish. Begin by removing any hardware and tracing the box outline on paper—top, sides, front and back. Draw the design shown or one you've devised yourself. Cut the ve-

INLAY BOX

TOP VENEER is glued to box with tape side up, using slip-sheet. Brown or wax paper between veneer and box is removed as veneer is positioned.

TOOLS YOU'LL need include a model knife equipped with fine blades; steel rule to cut against; a square; veneer roller; and a veneer saw.

TOP OF BOX is pressed down with a veneer roller immediately after veneer has been positioned to insure a secure bond over entire glued area.

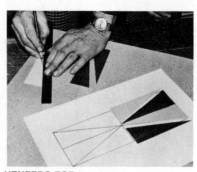

VENEERS FOR top design are cut to size with a model knife. Light veneer is aspen and dark is mahogany. Place pieces on pattern to check fit.

OVERHANGING VENEER is cut off with a veneer saw. Later it's sanded smooth. The extra overhang is added at the corners to insure a smooth edge.

neer sections for the top exactly to size with a model knife and tape them together.

Glue the assembled design (make sure joints are tight) to the box—taped side up—with contact adhesive. To assure proper veneer placement (you can't move it once it's down), put a sheet of brown wrapping paper or wax paper between the box top and the veneer, leaving a slight margin at the front. Align the front veneer and box edges, press the veneer in place, then gradually slip the sheet away. Then roll the veneer firmly and evenly.

Next mark and cut the veneer and border for the sides, lid and bottom, allowing an extra 1/16 in. to overhang at each corner. Tape the veneer and inlay together and glue them to the box using the slip-sheet method just described. Go over the veneer with a roller and trim the overhangs.

Mark, cut, tape and glue the front and back veneers in the same way, again allowing a 1/16-in. overhang that is trimmed off. To finish the box,

first peel off your tape. A razor blade used carefully helps. Sand the surface smooth, then wipe it with a tack cloth and carefully apply a finish of your choice.

TRAY

You can make a striking grain design as on this tray top by using two pieces of veneer taped together. Materials you'll need are a piece of 1/2-in. plywood good on both sides for the core of the tray (10 x 15 in. or whatever size you wish), veneer for the tray top (we used African Bubinga) and tray bottom (a less expensive plain mahogany is fine here), 1/2 x 1 1/4-in. cherry or other wood edging strips to size; veneer tape and tung oil.

Tools and equipment needed include a model knife, metal straightedge, plastic resin or yellow glue, short-nap roller, file and sandpaper in grits from 60 to 400. Either glue requires a veneer press made by sandwiching the tray between wax

TRAY

JOINING VENEERS makes it possible to create patterns in the grain. Set up your patterns by joining veneer sections with short pieces of tape across the joint and add one long horizontal strip.

APPLY PLASTIC RESIN, such as Weldwood, with a thin-nap roller to be sure the glue is evenly applied over all the surface. Any area not covered may cause a bump. Work quickly after you apply the resin.

TOP AND BOTTOM veneer edges all have been taped to plywood and the tray is now ready for the press.

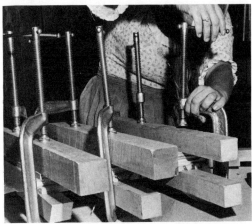

TO MAKE PRESS, use three hardwood 2x2s, birch plywood and wax paper on each side. Hold with C-clamps.

paper, two sheets of plywood the same size as the tray and three 2x2s on either side. Six C-clamps hold the assembly together in a modified veneer press while the glue dries.

Begin by cutting the veneers for the tray top and bottom the same size as the plywood piece. Cut the veneer so its grain is at right angles to the top layer of plywood to help prevent warping. Tape veneers together with short crosspieces, then with one long vertical strip.

Next apply plastic resin evenly to the back of the veneer that goes on the tray top, facing the tape side up. Now work quickly until the tray is in the press. Place the veneer on the plywood and tape the edges. Glue and tape the tray bottom veneer.

Place the tray in the press with wax paper on each side and start applying pressure with the C-clamps, working from the middle out. After you've turned down all clamps part way, begin from the middle again and tighten them as much as possible. Wait about 12 hours; then remove the tray and peel off the tape. Align veneer and plywood edges.

Sand with the grain, clean, then rub on tung oil. Glue and press the long edging pieces to the tray with bar clamps. Then do the same to the short edgings, round the corners, sand and finish with tung oil.

BACKGAMMON BOARD

This backgammon board is made with four wood veneers and inlay banding. Materials you'll need are four pieces of ½ x 14 x 17-in. birch plywood good on two sides (two pieces each for the board and a press), wood strips to make the box and inner compartments, edging for plywood, two 3-in. butt hinges, a box catch, plastic resin or yellow glue, sandpaper from coarse to fine grit; masking tape and tung oil.

You need light and dark veneers for the playing triangles, another for the center of the board face and board back, a fourth for the inner compartments, plus inlay banding.

Tools needed are a plane, glue roller, table saw, sharp model knife, four bar clamps and a press. The veneer press, although larger, is used as it was in the preceding project. It's made of eight 2x2s, two plywood sheets, two layers of wax paper and eight C-clamps.

Cutting and taping veneer

Mark the veneer layout for the face and back of the backgammon board on two pieces of plywood. Each side of the boards must be completely veneered to prevent warpage. *Be sure to set up a right and left-hand panel with alternating colored triangles.*

Make cardboard templates of the veneer triangles and draw outlines on the veneer. The latter may need trimming later, so make templates slightly larger than required. The jig shown can help you cut the veneer with a model knife. Use moderate pressure and make repeated passes over the veneer. To plane the veneer, brush it lightly with the grain across the plane's cutting edge.

Cut all veneer pieces. Inlay bands can be cut and taped now or glued later in a space cut and chipped out of the veneer after it's pressed.

You can begin taping the face pieces together with short crosspieces of tape pulled tightly. Then tape the joints lengthwise, covering the cross tapings. Tape the face veneers for both panels, then tape both back inlay and veneers.

Mix the plastic resin and smooth some on a plywood panel; then place the back veneer on the panel (tape side up) and tape edges. Place veneered side down in the press on wax paper; then glue and tape edges of the face veneer to top side of the panel. Cover with wax paper, plywood and the top 2x2s evenly spaced; then apply pressure with C-clamps.

After the proper glue-setting time has elapsed, remove the panel and repeat the process for the second panel. Remove the tape, sand the panels with the grain and oil lightly.

Constructing the box

Cut the ¾x1¼-in. pieces and make lap joints. Glue them together; then clamp and glue them to faces of the panels using bar clamps and eight C-clamps as in the photo. Use wax paper and scrap wood between the board and clamps.

Cut, glue and clamp the edging to the plywood panels, make the box compartments and hinge the box parts together. Sand, chip away any excess glue and lightly oil the box.

MULTIPIECE VENEER PROJECTS

Use two mirrors hinged together with tape to help visualize a completed multipiece veneer assembly such as the hexagonal tabletop shown. Position the mirrors at 90° angle to reflect a four-piece match. Shift the mirrors to 60°, 45° and 22½° to visualize a 6, 8 and 16-piece match, respectively.

Once you find the desired match, mark pencil lines along the inside edges of the mirrors. Cut out the veneer pieces using a veneer saw or utility knife guided by a straightedge or hardboard template. Then tape the veneer pieces together with gummed veneer tape and, trimming the overhanging veneer edges, moisten the veneer tape and remove it with a cabinet scraper.

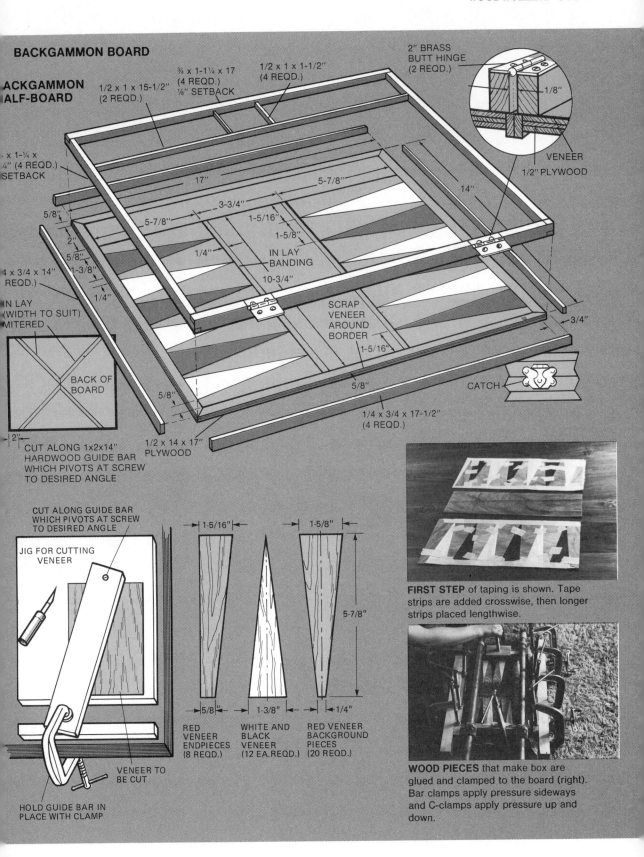

BACKGAMMON BOARD

ACKGAMMON ALF-BOARD

1/2 x 1 x 15-1/2" (2 REQD.)

¾ x 1-¼ x 17 (4 REQD.) ⅛" SETBACK

1/2 x 1 x 1-1/2" (4 REQD.)

2" BRASS BUTT HINGE (2 REQD.)

1/8"

VENEER

1/2" PLYWOOD

x 1-¼ x ¼" (4 REQD.) SETBACK

17"

5-7/8"

14"

5/8"

2"

5/8"

1-3/8"

3-3/4"

5-7/8"

1-5/16"

1-5/8"

1/4"

IN LAY BANDING

10-3/4"

4 x ¾ x 14" REQD.)

1/4"

N LAY (WIDTH TO SUIT) MITERED

SCRAP VENEER AROUND BORDER

1-5/16"

3/4"

BACK OF BOARD

5/8"

5/8"

CATCH

2"

CUT ALONG 1x2x14" HARDWOOD GUIDE BAR WHICH PIVOTS AT SCREW TO DESIRED ANGLE

1/2 x 14 x 17" PLYWOOD

1/4 x 3/4 x 17-1/2" (4 REQD.)

CUT ALONG GUIDE BAR WHICH PIVOTS AT SCREW TO DESIRED ANGLE

1-5/16"

1-5/8"

5-7/8"

JIG FOR CUTTING VENEER

5/8"

1-3/8"

1/4"

RED VENEER ENDPIECES (8 REQD.)

WHITE AND BLACK VENEER (12 EA. REQD.)

RED VENEER BACKGROUND PIECES (20 REQD.)

HOLD GUIDE BAR IN PLACE WITH CLAMP

VENEER TO BE CUT

FIRST STEP of taping is shown. Tape strips are added crosswise, then longer strips placed lengthwise.

WOOD PIECES that make box are glued and clamped to the board (right). Bar clamps apply pressure sideways and C-clamps apply pressure up and down.

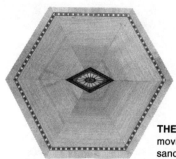

THE COMPLETED TABLETOP after removing trimming tape and then finish-sanding. Allow about 48 hours before applying finish.

HOLD TWO MIRRORS AT A 60° ANGLE to reflect a six-piece veneer match. Then mark pencil lines along the inside mirror edges.

USE A HARDBOARD TEMPLATE to cut six veneer pieces. Make a small cut in veneer edge to prevent splintering as the knife exits.

ASSEMBLE THE PIECES into a hexagon shape using gummed veneer tape. If cut accurately, the last piece will fit without trimming.

TAPE THE DIAMOND-SHAPED INLAY motif to the veneer assembly for use as a template when cutting out the center area with a knife.

CUT AND TAPE THE BORDER INLAY STRIPS in place. Align a steel straightedge with the veneer joints to cut tight-fitting miters.

APPLY VENEER GLUE to the hexagonal assembly and to the tabletop, which is made from ¾-in. fir plywood edged in hardwood.

SEPARATE GLUED SURFACES with wax paper to permit positioning veneer exactly. Remove the paper and press down the veneer.

DECORATIVE WALNUT BOX

This attractive box is accented with a floral design overlay top veneer and an inlay veneer border. Both of these veneers are typical examples of the many ready-made veneers available for enhancing your woodworking projects.

First, cut four box sides and bottom from ½-in. walnut. Make the box top, which receives the overlay veneer, from ½-in. birch plywood edged with ½ x ½-in. walnut.

Use veneer glue to apply the floral design overlay veneer. To prevent the veneer from shifting while clamping pressure is applied, drive two ½-in.-long brads into the veneer. After the glue dries, set the brad heads slightly, then fill the holes with walnut-colored wood putty.

Next, apply veneer to the underside of the box top to counterbalance any expansion or contraction in the top veneer that could cause warping. Then shape the top's edges with a ⁵⁄₃₂-in. roman

THE FINISHED WALNUT BOX is enhanced by the use of ready-made floral design overlay veneer and the unique inlay borders.

ogee bit. Cut a shallow groove in the box bottom's edges on a table saw to receive the inlay border. Glue the border in place with yellow woodworking glue.

MAKE THE BOX TOP from ½-in. birch plywood edged with ½ x ½-in. walnut. Glue and tape the edging to the plywood top.

APPLY GLUE TO THE VENEER. If it is wavy, use woodworking glue. Apply glue to both surfaces and clamp quickly.

CUT SHALLOW GROOVES in the box-bottom edges on a table saw for the inlay border strips. Install strips with glue only.

SHAPE DECORATIVE BOX-TOP EDGES using a router fitted with a ⁵⁄₃₂-in. roman ogee bit. Finish-sand the top with 220-grit paper.

REMOVE PROTECTIVE PAPER from the veneer by moistening it slightly, then scraping it with a wide chisel or cabinet scraper.

DOOR WITH WALNUT CROTCH INLAY

Here's a clever way to make unique custom cabinet doors featuring two veneers of different wood species. We used book-matched walnut crotch veneer for the center inlay and contrasting butternut veneer for the border. Apply the veneers to a ¾-in. fir plywood door panel edged with hardwood.

First, tape together two matching crotch veneer pieces. Next, cut a full-size hardboard template of the center inlay. Use the template to cut out the center of a sheet of paper. Position the paper "window" on the crotch veneer, selecting the most desirable wood grain pattern for the inlay.

Mark the paper's corner locations with masking tape. Tape the butternut veneer over the walnut crotch veneer and use a utility knife to cut through both veneers at the same time. Tape the walnut inlay to the center of the butternut veneer border and apply the veneers as a single unit to the door panel using veneer glue.

BUTT TWO WALNUT CROTCH VENEER PIECES together in a book match design. Trim the mating edges to form a tight-fitting joint.

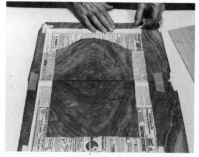

MARK THE PAPER WINDOW CORNER LOCATIONS with masking tape. Position the window so the most attractive wood grain shows.

TAPE THE BUTTERNUT VENEER to the walnut veneer using the tape corners as guides. Butternut veneer will form door border.

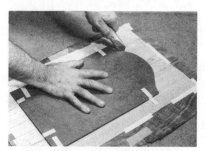

TAPE A HARDBOARD TEMPLATE in place and cut through both veneers at once. Firm pressure on template will prevent shifting.

REMOVE BUTTERNUT CENTER CUTOUT and the outer walnut border. Tape together the walnut inlay and the butternut border.

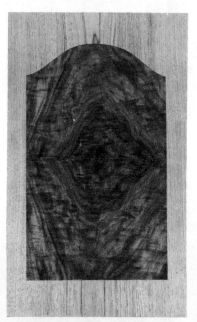

A WALNUT CROTCH INLAY is surrounded by a contrasting butternut veneer border on the completed cabinet door.

VENEER THE DOOR PANEL BACKSIDE to counterbalance any expansion or contraction of the face veneers that might cause warping.

APPLY THE FACE VENEER to the door panel with veneer glue. Use a veneer roller to ensure 100 percent surface contact.

Cloth tape inlays

■ AT FIRST GLANCE, the colorful design on the lid of this trinket box looks like expensive enameled inlay work. Actually it's nothing more than patterned fabric tape cemented in shallow channels and coated with a clear plastic finish, but the simulation is nearly perfect.

Any fancy cloth tape, ¼ to 1-in. wide, can be used this way; a metallic braid will produce a handsome inlay of delicately wrought gold bands.

The picture sequence shows how you first create $\frac{1}{32}$-in.-deep channels for the tape with a router and chisel. Then you miter the tape like the corners of a picture frame with a 45° template and a wood chisel, after which you apply white glue sparingly to the channels and press the tape in place flush with the surface.

Finally, you finish both box lid and cloth tape with two coats of a transparent urethane to enhance the wood grain and bring out the beauty of the tape pattern.

SHALLOW CHANNELS are first routed to equal thickness of the tape, then corners are squared.

ENDS OF TAPE are mitered by holding sharp wood chisel against 45° template and cutting over hardboard.

WHITE GLUE is spread evenly in channels, then tape is pressed in place. Wipe excess glue with damp cloth.

WHEN GLUE is dry, tape is given two coats of clear urethane finish. Then the wood is coated.

Bird-carving secrets

■ WOODCARVING EXPERTS can create birds so real that some people think they are stuffed birds, while others may think that real feathers are glued to the wood body.

Most of these experts agree that there is more to creating a bird than carving. Much of their time is spent in research, studying pictures and actual birds. Although most of the birds are carved from basswood, a light wood that is sometimes hollowed to make it even lighter, a knowledge of metalwork is also needed. Most carvings have metal feet and legs, and metal is used to make parts of the bird's environment. Assembling the bird—gluing individually carved feathers, attaching the feet and balancing the bird in

CARVING A 22-IN.-HIGH GREAT HORNED OWL. Later this bird mounted on a section of hollow tree trunk.

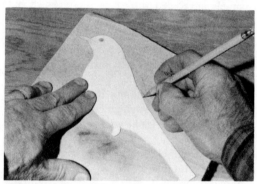

BEGIN BY OUTLINING a pattern on basswood; the beak runs with the grain.

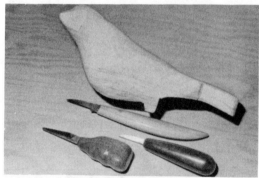

CUT OUT THE ROUGH SHAPE with a bandsaw. Begin to round areas as needed.

CARVE OUT AREAS to shape the bird and draw in each individual feather.

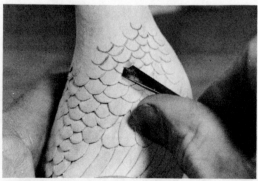

OUTLINE FEATHERS with a modeler's knife. Begin carving with skew chisel at tail.

its setting—is part of each project. Treating the birds with oil paint in natural colors means a careful mixing of paints to get the right hues.

The most popular of these carved birds are the familiar ones—cardinals, chickadees and wrens. Game birds as well as songbirds also have strong appeal.

The time it takes an expert to carve a bird ranges from a week (about 80 hours) for a robin, to two or three months (300 to 400 hours) for an owl, pheasant or other large bird. This includes painstaking attention to detail.

The advice experts consider most important for novice wood carvers is to study birds as much as possible. Get pictures of birds, watch them and note how they move and hold themselves. Serious carvers would benefit by borrowing study skins—birds that are stuffed but not mounted—from schools or museums. They suggest carving a bird from a composite of pictures and information.

The mistake most often made by carvers, according to the experts, is in shaping the bird's head and bill. Often the back part of the bill isn't narrowed enough. Follow photos closely and gradually taper the bill from front to back. Another common error is misshapen feet—a pitfall some experts avoid by using metal feet.

THERE ARE 450 individual feathers on this purple gallinule. He feeds in a plastic-resin pond with lilies carved of wood. His feet are metal.

BURN central feather shaft and barbs on both sides with an electric pencil.

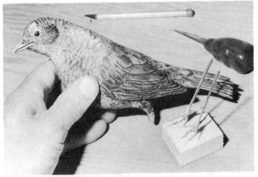

BIRD is completely burned and ready to paint. Front leg wires attach to base.

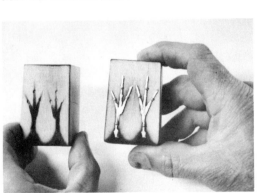

TO MAKE FEET, pour molten metal in a wood mold held in a vise. Legs are wire.

REAL OR NOT? It's hard to determine as this robin perches in tall grass.

DISPLAYED IN THEIR NATURAL ENVIRONMENT, birds look even more realistic. Two bluebirds make their home on the bough of a blossoming tree. Although most birds are life-size, these flying widgeons (bottom left) are one-third size. Water is made of plastic resin, and grass that bends in the wind is wood. Wings of the colorful yellow-shafted flicker (above right) are separate wood pieces.

Carve these sea gulls in flight

■ WITH A HAND-HELD power tool you don't have to be a master carver to make these handsome sea gulls.

1. Draw the pattern. Make a full-scale drawing of the sea gull. Transfer the outline to basswood or other soft wood. Use 1½ in.-thick wood for the bodies and ⅜-in.-thick wood for the wings.

2. Cut out the pieces. With a jigsaw cut out the pieces. Bevel-cut the wings at a 15° angle.

3. Glue the wings to the body. Apply white glue to mating surfaces and wait until glue gets tacky. Then press parts together.

4. Shape the bird. Use the drum sander attach-ment in the power tool to shape the bird. Bore a hole the diameter of coathanger wire in the bottom of each bird.

5. Apply finish. First brush white alkyd primer on the birds and base. When dry apply an oil stain. Make highlights while stain is wet by rubbing with a turpentine-soaked rag.

Bore holes in the base for the attaching wires. Cut coathanger wire to 5-, 6- and 7-in. lengths; attach birds to the base.

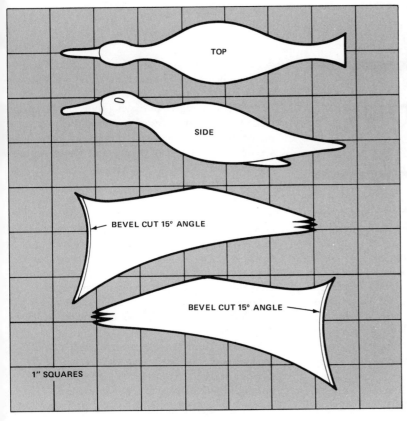

TOP

SIDE

BEVEL CUT 15° ANGLE

BEVEL CUT 15° ANGLE

1" SQUARES

CUT OUT the three pieces.

GLUE PIECES and let them dry.

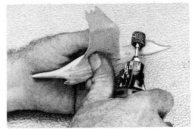

SHAPE BIRDS with a hand power tool.

Woodcarving projects

■ CARVING AND FINISHING even a simple object is one of the most satisfying forms of woodworking.

Many carvings are made with just two basic types of tools: gouges and chisels. Gouges are made of steel that is curved to varying degrees to "gouge" out excess wood. A "quick" gouge has a very deep curve that's intended especially for use in deep and rough cutting. "Slow" gouges have flatter curves and are used in finishing work. Widths at the cutting edge of these tools can vary from 1/16 to 5/8 inch.

Chisels are beveled on both sides and used by carvers to cut in designs and clean out wood in detailed areas during the finishing stages. Their ends can be square or skew (angled) in widths to accommodate rough or fine work.

Your first purchase of carving tools should include three or four sizes of gouges and chisels, a mallet to drive the tools, clamps or carver's screws to secure your work, and sharpening stones.

SNACK DISH

Scooping out this handy dish is a good way to become familiar with your carving tools and how to handle them. You'll need a 9 × 6 × 1¼-in. block of wood. Mahogany or walnut both have fairly even grain and finish nicely. Very sharp tools will make your carving easier and safer.

Tools: 1-in. fantail gouge, 5/8-in. bent gouge, 5/8-in. skew chisel, wood mallet and bandsaw or other saw.

Method: Draw the dish design either directly on the wood or on paper and transfer it. This design is a freehand "avocado" shape with part of the rim slightly thicker to serve as a handle.

Note: In this and the following projects the

TOOLS USED are (from bottom): fantail gouge, bent gouge, skew chisel and wood mallet.

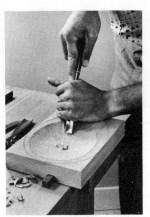

THE RIGHT HAND exerts pressure and the left hand guides as the bent gouge gives texture.

THE WOODEN MALLET exerts extra pressure on the fantail gouge as the dish is shaped.

THE SKEW CHISEL is used for chip-carving of the finishing triangle decoration.

wood should be securely fastened to a worktable so you can work with both hands safely behind the cutting edge of the tool.

With the fantail gouge (the working end of this gouge is fanned out) and wood mallet, hollow out the dish. Then with the bent gouge finish hollowing and giving texture to the inside of the dish. (This gouge is actually bent and was designed to hollow shallow areas.)

Next, saw or use a gouge to remove excess wood. Work so that the sides are cupped inward toward the bottom. Then turn the dish over, secure it, and with the gouge shape and give the outside texture.

Last, the finishing decoration, a series of triangles, is carved on the dish top. Draw the number of triangles you wish as in the illustration. Then cut along the center lines with a skew chisel held vertically, tapering the cut from ⅛ in. at the center (B) to nothing at the triangle tips. Cut A to B, B to C and B to D. Remove the waste, tapering and paring the wood away from the sides to the center. Pare A to C, A to D and C to D.

TRINKET BOX

Here's a walnut trinket box with a low-relief flower design. For this you need a 4½ × 3½ × 8-in. block.

Tools: ⅝-in. flat straight gouge, ⅝-in. bent gouge, ⅝-in. skew chisel, mallet, 1-in. carpenter's chisel, bandsaw and coping saw.

Method: Make sure the wood is square, then with a circular saw or bandsaw halve it along the 4½-in. depth to make the box and lid. Go over the box with a flat gouge to give it texture. The box legs are ⅞ × 1¼ × ¼-in. deep. Mark off the first two dimensions and cut along marks to a ¼-in. depth with a coping saw. Remove excess wood

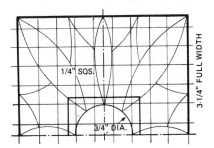

TOOLS USED are (from bottom): straight gouge, bent gouge, skew chisel, mallet and slipstone.

BOX LEGS are marked and sawed to a ¼-in. depth. Here excess wood is being gouged out.

INSIDE OF THE BOX is hollowed with a bent gouge to a 1-⅜-in. depth, leaving a ¼-in. lip on the edge.

SHAPE THE three levels on the lid. Texture and beveled corners are made on the lowest level.

THE FLOWER design is drawn, then incised with a chisel; excess wood is then chiseled away.

with a carpenter's chisel or gouge. Mark inner space to be hollowed out, leaving a ¼-in. lip. With mallet and bent gouge, scoop out the interior to a 1⅜-in. depth.

Inside the box lid make a ¼-in.-wide by ⅛-in.-deep lip with a skew chisel. Find the center of the outside of the lid. Mark off a 1-in. square for the knob and a 2¼ × 3¼ in. rectangle for the flower petal area. Using a ⅝-in. straight gouge and mallet, level the area outside the rectangle sloping down to the corners. With the same gouge, level the petal area about ¾ in; draw the petal design.

With skew chisel, round the knob, incise petal lines and cut away petal background. Texture the lid with a flat gouge. Finish with oil.

PARTRIDGE MIRROR

Our "partridges in a pear tree" mirror was carved from a single piece of white pine.

Materials: White pine board, 1¼ × 11 × 14½ in.; mirror, 6½ × 9½ in.; glazier's points or ½-in. brads; brown wrapping paper; white glue; hanging device.

Tools: ⅜-in. flat, straight gouge; ⅝-in. flat, straight gouge; ¼-in. quick, straight gouge (remember "quick" means the end has a deep curve); ⅝-in. skew chisel; mallet; jigsaw.

Method: Begin with a smooth, flat board with square corners. Draw the frame including the 5¾ × 8¾-in. center mirror area on paper and transfer it to the wood. Saw the frame outline with a jigsaw. With the skew chisel, silhouette the

TOOLS NEEDED: ⅜ and ⅝-in. flat gouges, quick gouge, chisel and mallet.

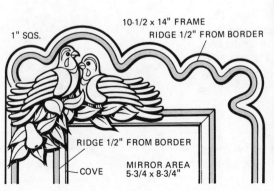

1" SQS.

10-1/2 x 14" FRAME
RIDGE 1/2" FROM BORDER

RIDGE 1/2" FROM BORDER

COVE

MIRROR AREA
5-3/4 x 8-3/4"

MAKE ridge ½-in. from inner border.

CUT THE design along drawn lines.

birds. They are on the highest plane. Using the ⅝-in. flat gouge and mallet, reduce the depth of the rest of the frame about ¼ in. Remove the center mirror area with a jigsaw.

Mark off, then remove with a ⅜-in. flat gouge a ridge about ½ in. within the outer border and a second ridge ½ in. away from the inner border where the mirror will be placed. With the ⅝-in. gouge make a cove ⅛-in. away from the second ridge toward the mirror area.

Next, define the partridge detail with the skew chisel. Cut along the lines already drawn.

On the back, mark off ¾ in. around the inner frame perimeter for the rabbet that will hold the mirror and cardboard backing. With a skew chisel (you can cheat by using a router), remove the wood to accommodate the mirror and backing (½-in. depth).

After sanding the surfaces smooth, apply stain and oil finish to the frame.

Place the mirror and cardboard backing in the rabbet and secure them with glazier's points or ½-in. brads. Then dampen brown wrapping paper slightly larger than the mirror frame and glue it to the back. When the glue becomes tacky, trim the paper ¼ in. from the border with a utility knife. As the paper dries, it will shrink and provide a smooth backing. Finally, add the hanging device.

Hint: You might first practice gouging and cutting scrap wood.

CAT

Carving in the round will test your ability to visualize a three-dimensional object. Our lifelike cat was carved from a 6¼ × 6¼ × 11-in. mahogany block.

Tools: You'll need a 1-in. fantail gouge; ⅝-in. bent gouge; ⅝-in. flat, straight gouge; ⅝-in. skew chisel; ¼-in. quick, straight gouge; mallet; wood rasp and bandsaw.

Note: You might get a clearer idea of how your finished piece should look if you make a clay model before you begin carving. It also helps to secure the bottom of your block of wood to the worktable with carver's screws, or by running screws through a piece of plywood and the wood block and clamping the plywood to the work surface. Doing so allows you to see all sides of the object and work on it in an upright position.

Method: Sketch the side views (A) of the cat on the wood block. Then cut away the waste with a bandsaw. Sketch the front view (B) of the cat and do the same.

TOOLS YOU NEED for this project (from the bottom): 1-in. fantail gouge, ⅝-in. bent gouge, ⅝-in. flat gouge, ⅝-in. skew chisel, ¼-in. quick gouge and wood mallet.

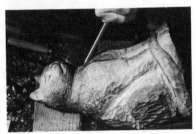

WORK ON the cat's neck is done with a ¼-in. quick gouge.

SAW ON DOTTED LINES

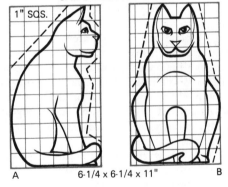

A   6-1/4 x 6-1/4 x 11"   B

C

A SMOOTH FINISH is one key to producing this sleek, lifelike cat.

As you work, it will help to draw in guide lines. With the 1-in. fantail gouge and mallet, continue to remove the excess wood and begin making rough details (C). A center line drawn down the cat's front will help you keep the proportions.

Begin to refine the details. The ⅝-in. bent gouge is good for rounding areas like the cat's haunches. The ⅝-in. straight gouge can be used to smooth the gouge marks made by the fantail gouge, and to further refine details. Use the skew chisel to outline and make small details like the cat's mouth and paws. The ¼-in. quick gouge can be used to define small places like the neck, tail and between the legs.

Remember, whenever you must exert a great amount of force, your tools probably need sharpening—either with a slipstone or with both oilstone and slipstone.

Smooth the cat with a wood rasp followed by three grades of sandpaper. Apply three or more coats of linseed oil, allow 24 hours between coats, and finish with butcher's wax.

Often the simple action of a carving tool on wood acts as a burnisher. When the tools serve as a burnisher you may want to leave your work in its natural state without applying a finish. Before burnishing, strop the tools on a piece of leather containing a mixture of emery powder and petroleum jelly, immediately after they've been sharpened.

Another simple way of burnishing a carving is by rubbing it with wood shavings.

FINISHES FOR WOOD CARVINGS

Newly cut timber that will attract dirt and grease should be sealed. Several coats of white French polish applied with a soft brush and rubbed down with fine steel wool will seal it and leave a slight gloss.

Or you might choose to give a carving several coats of linseed oil. It can be burnished with beeswax applied with a coarse cloth.

The soft luster of wood doesn't lend itself to lacquering, varnishing or finishing with a method that gives a high gloss. But distressing of softwoods can make an interesting finish.

One method of distressing wood is to burn the surface slightly with a blow torch and later brush the wood in one direction with a steel brush. This treatment highlights the harder growth of the wood and improves the form of the object, but it should not be used with very resinous timbers or woods containing large knots.

Another method of distressing softwood is to poke holes in it with an awl or ice pick. This is generally followed by a dark stain for an effect like wormwood.

Use a good furniture polish occasionally to protect the finish.

Interlocking wood sculpture—an ancient art

BASE FOR CANDY OR
HORS D'OEUVRE DISH

DECORATIVE CANDLE BASE

INTRIGUING SCULPTURE is a grand exercise in woodworking, and produces a finished product that can be used functionally (above) or simply as a conversation piece. Work with a piece of well-seasoned hardwood such as walnut or maple.

WALL DISPLAY

1. AFTER SELECTING stock, clamp wood in the vise and rough-shape it round using a chisel and plane.

2. ROUGH-HEWN BLOCK is then mounted in a lathe and turned to true size—4 in. dia. by 7 in. long.

3. FOR ACCURACY, a large centerhole is bored on the lathe. If drill press is used, clamp the workpiece.

■ YOUR FRIENDS are certain to marvel at this fascinating carved-wood sculpture. And they'll be curious to know just how you created it. Actually, the concept is based on the hand carvings made in the bazaars of India and elsewhere in the East by native craftsmen using primitive tools. Unlike them, you can use power tools to remove the waste wood quickly and almost effortlessly.

Making the link is a welcome change from the disciplines of precise measurement and accurate working so necessary for most sophisticated workshop projects. The finished sculpture is attractive as an art piece or it can be put to work as a dish or candy base.

It will pay you to select well-seasoned hardwood for this project. Walnut or maple are good choices because both are strong, yet not too tough to carve. After selecting stock to use, rough-round it by sawing, chiseling and planing. Next, shape the block to a cylinder by turning on the lathe.

The large hole through the center can be bored (in from both ends) in the lathe, by bench drill, or, most laboriously, by hand with an expansive or center bit in a brace.

Next, wrap a piece of paper around the wood and carefully mark and cut away any overlap to leave edges that just meet. Mark out the lattice-work shape shown in the diagram using light pencil lines initially; then, after checking, boldly line in the bars with a felt-tip pen. Secure the paper to the wood with white glue or library paste. When it's dry, most of the waste wood can be removed by chain-drilling a series of holes with the cylinder resting on a channel-section stand. When you're drilling, *it is important* to judge that the center line of the bar adjacent to each hole being drilled is precisely in the "top dead center" position. This assures that the holes in each side of the bars will be parallel down through the thickness of the cylinder walls. The uneven edges left by the drilling can be smoothed with a sharp chisel and penknife.

Grip the wood on end in the vise and saw halfway through the thickness of the cylinder

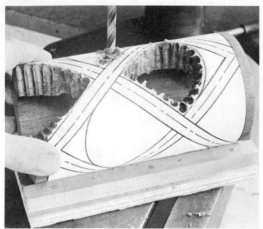

4. MOST OF the waste wood is removed by chain-drilling. Notice the support stand beneath the wood.

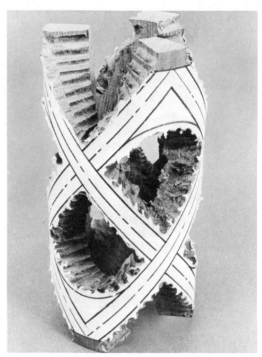

5. CYLINDER looks like this when waste has been drilled away. Drilling must be vertically accurate.

wall (underpass bars) each side of the *overpass* bars (see photo No. 6.) Pare away the waste wood in such a way that each *underpass* bar descends to the halfway position against each *overpass* bar.

It will now be obvious that similar—though more difficult—paring is required inside the cylinder to shape the inner surfaces of the overpass bars to clear the underpass ones.

A fret or piercing saw is used to saw through between the underpass and overpass bars where they cross as shown in step No. 8. The three separated, but interlocked, pieces are now easier to deal with as the bars are made roughly round or elliptical in section by careful whittling with a chisel or penknife. The points at one end can be shaped inward to give a horn-shaped single point support most suitable if the sculpture is used as a

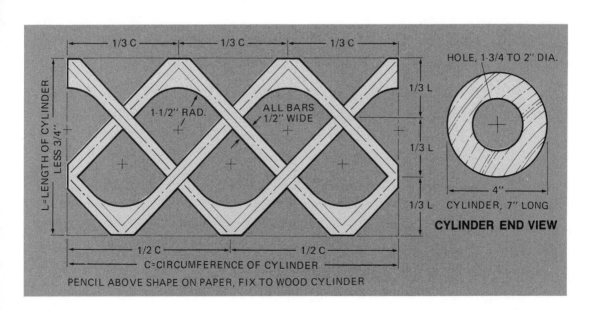

1/3 C — 1/3 C — 1/3 C

HOLE, 1-3/4 TO 2" DIA.

L=LENGTH OF CYLINDER LESS 3/4"

1-1/2" RAD.

ALL BARS 1/2" WIDE

1/3 L

1/3 L

1/3 L

4"

CYLINDER, 7" LONG

1/2 C — 1/2 C

C=CIRCUMFERENCE OF CYLINDER

CYLINDER END VIEW

PENCIL ABOVE SHAPE ON PAPER, FIX TO WOOD CYLINDER

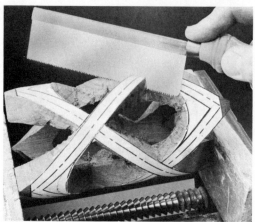

6. WOOD IS GRIPPED on end in vise, and backsaw is used to saw halfway through the underpass bars.

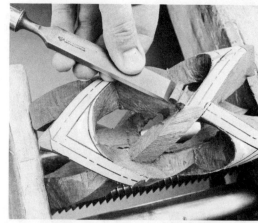

7. WITH WORK still in the vise, upper surfaces of the underpass bars are then chiseled away.

base for a dish. With the sculpture arranged in its natural resting position, the base ends can be carved or sanded to give an area of contact with the surface under them.

Final smoothing is made by diligent use of medium-grade, then fine-grade glass or garnet paper. The carving can be finished with two or three coats of shellac or varnish applied with a soft brush. Each coat, including the last, should be lightly rubbed with steel wool. After the last coat apply a little wax polish to bring out the full beauty of the grain and your carving.

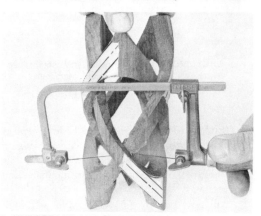

8. UNDERPASS AND OVERPASS bars are separated with a fine-bladed saw. Bars are now easier to work.

CUSTOMARY TO METRIC (CONVERSION)
Conversion factors can be carried so far they become impractical. In cases below where an entry is exact it is followed by an asterisk (*). Where considerable rounding off has taken place, the entry is followed by a + or a − sign.

Linear Measure

inches	millimeters
1/16	1.5875*
1/8	3.2
3/16	4.8
1/4	6.35*
5/16	7.9
3/8	9.5
7/16	11.1
1/2	12.7*
9/16	14.3
5/8	15.9
11/16	17.5
3/4	19.05*
13/16	20.6
7/8	22.2
15/16	23.8
1	25.4*

inches	centimeters
1	2.54*
2	5.1
3	7.6
4	10.2
5	12.7*
6	15.2
7	17.8
8	20.3
9	22.9
10	25.4*
11	27.9
12	30.5

feet	centimeters	meters
1	30.48*	.3048*
2	61	.61
3	91	.91
4	122	1.22
5	152	1.52
6	183	1.83
7	213	2.13
8	244	2.44
9	274	2.74
10	305	3.05
50	1524*	15.24*
100	3048*	30.48*

1 yard = .9144* meters
1 rod = 5.0292* meters
1 mile = 1.6 kilometers
1 nautical mile = 1.852* kilometers

Weights

ounces	grams
1	28.3
2	56.7
3	85
4	113
5	142
6	170
7	198
8	227
9	255
10	283
11	312
12	340
13	369
14	397
15	425
16	454

Formula (exact):
ounces × 28.349 523 125* = grams

pounds	kilograms
1	.45
2	.9
3	1.4
4	1.8
5	2.3
6	2.7
7	3.2
8	3.6
9	4.1
10	4.5

1 short ton (2000 lbs) = 907 kilograms (kg)
Formula (exact):
pounds × .453 592 37* = kilograms

Fluid Measure

(Milliliters [ml] and cubic centimeters [cc] are equivalent, but it is customary to use milliliters for liquids.)

1 cu in	=	16.39 ml
1 fl oz	=	29.6 ml
1 cup	=	237 ml
1 pint	=	473 ml
1 quart	=	946 ml
	=	.946 liters
1 gallon	=	3785 ml
	=	3.785 liters

Formula (exact):
fluid ounces × 29.573 529 562 5* = milliliters

Volume

1 cu in	=	16.39 cubic centimeters (cc)
1 cu ft	=	28 316.7 cc
1 bushel	=	35 239.1 cc
1 peck	=	8 809.8 cc

Area

1 sq in	=	6.45 sq cm
1 sq ft	=	929 sq cm
	=	.093 sq meters
1 sq yd	=	.84 sq meters
1 acre	=	4 046.9 sq meters
	=	.404 7 hectares
1 sq mile	=	2 589 988 sq meters
	=	259 hectares
	=	2.589 9 sq kilometers

Miscellaneous

1 British thermal unit (Btu) (mean) = 1 055.9 joules
1 horsepower = 745.7 watts
= .75 kilowatts
caliber (diameter of a firearm's bore in hundredths of an inch) = .254 millimeters (mm)

1 atmosphere pressure = 101 325* pascals (newtons per sq meter)
1 pound per square inch (psi) = 6 895 pascals
1 pound per square foot = 47.9 pascals
1 knot = 1.85 kilometers per hour
1 mile per hour = 1.6093 kilometers per hour